DANIEL GALMICHE

FRENCH BRASSERIE COOKBOOK

THE HEART OF FRENCH HOME COOKING

dbp

DUNCAN BAIRD PUBLISHERS

LONDON

FRENCH BRASSERIE
COOKBOOK

Daniel Galmiche

Distributed in the USA and Canada by
Sterling Publishing Co., Inc.
387 Park Avenue South, New York, NY 10016-8810

First published in the UK and USA in 2011 by
Duncan Baird Publishers Ltd.
Sixth Floor, Castle House, 75–76 Wells Street
London W1T 3QH

Managing Editor: Grace Cheetham
Editors: Camilla Davis and Nicole Bator
French Consultant: Séverine Jeauneau
Managing Designer: Manisha Patel
Production: Uzma Taj
Commissioned Photography: Yuki Sugiura
Photography Assistant: Mick English
Food Stylists: Daniel Galmiche with Aya Nishimura
Prop Stylist: Wei Tang

Library of Congress Cataloging-in-Publication Data
available

ISBN: 978-1-84483-997-1

10 9 8 7 6 5 4 3 2 1

Typeset in ITC New Baskerville and MetaPlus
Colour reproduction by Colourscan, Singapore
Printed in China by Imago

For information about custom editions, special sales,
premium and corporate purchases, please contact
Sterling Special Sales Department at 800-805-5489 or
specialsales@sterlingpub.com.

PUBLISHER'S NOTE
While every care has been taken in compiling the recipes
for this book, Duncan Baird Publishers, or any other
persons who have been involved in working on this
publication, cannot accept responsibility for any errors
or omissions, inadvertent or not, that might be found
in the recipes or text, nor for any problems that might
arise as a result of preparing one of these recipes. If you
are pregnant or breastfeeding or have any special dietary
requirements or medical conditions, it is advisable
to consult a medical professional before following
any of the recipes contained in this book. Some wild
mushrooms can be fatally poisonous, however you cook
them. Neither the publisher nor the author can take
any responsibility for any illness or other unintended
consequences resulting from following any of the advice
or suggestions in this book.

NOTES ON THE RECIPES
Unless otherwise stated:
All recipes serve 4
Use medium fruit and vegetables
Use fresh ingredients, including herbs and chilies
Use large eggs
1 tsp. = 5ml 1 tbsp. = 15ml 1 cup = 240ml

Dedication

To three very special people: to my mom, Anne-Marie, and my late Great-Aunt Suzanne for their love and passion for cooking, which they passed on to me; to my first teacher, the late Yves Lalloz, who took me on when I was fifteen and guided me wisely through my three-year apprenticeship with him; and finally to my wife, Claire, for her charm, friendship and unconditional support, and my son, Antoine, whose love of life and food is contagious. My profound thanks to you all.

FOREWORD

Ever since my first wonderful meal at Harvey's in Bristol many years ago, I have been a great fan of Daniel's cooking. He is a true master of contemporary French cuisine and his passion, expertise, and attention to detail have ensured that dining at his table is never a disappointment. Who better, then, to teach the classics of the French kitchen?

The *French Brasserie Cookbook* contains all the recipes that you would expect, from Cheese Soufflé to Duck Rillettes, from Bouillabaisse to the perfect tarte tatin, but many of the classics have been given Daniel's unique twists. Alongside traditional onion soup, cassoulet, and Beef Bourguignon are Lime Risotto, Moules Marinières with Chilli and Lemongrass, and Coffee Crème Caramel. It's a fantastic combination of recipes and flavors.

And despite Daniel's huge talent as a Michelin-starred chef, this book is extremely accessible. It is practical, unfussy, and easy to use but, most satisfyingly, it is full of inspiring recipes that will immediately transport you to a French brasserie in your own home.

Heston Blumenthal

Contents

INTRODUCTION

What is it about brasseries?

I'm sitting on my balcony at home, musing on food as usual and asking myself what it is about brasseries we all love so much. So, I'm thinking ... you take a trip to Paris for a weekend and find yourself wandering happily through the wide boulevards, cobbled side streets and paved courtyards. You spot a stylish, yet unassuming, terrace and think you might sit outside and watch the world go by for an hour or so—but something draws you in. Is it the warm ambience and friendly faces? Is it the dark polished wood of the bar and ornate handles of the bar dispenser ready to serve you beer on tap? Is it the shining brass, the comfortable banquettes or the stunning art deco mirrors? Or is it quite simply the fantastic and mouthwatering smell of food drifting out of the kitchen? Whatever it is, it's irresistible.

As soon as you enter a brasserie in France, you are struck by a feeling of timelessness. You're ushered to a table by a *garçon de café* with a long, white apron, black bow tie and a quirky sense of humor. He seems to glide effortlessly amid the hustle and bustle of the busy interior and settles you into a cozy corner made more intimate by the stained-glass partition that boasts an elaborate hand-painted scene in the style of Toulouse Lautrec or a simple *fleur de lys*. You gaze around at the tarnished candlesticks and glamorous chandeliers and yet there is nothing grand or intimidating about being here— there's too much laughter and conviviality in the air for that. And it occurs to you brasseries are something of a paradox: sophisticated yet informal, chic yet unpretentious, boisterous yet elegant.

Popular for more than a century, brasseries are the fabled haunt of artists and writers, the meeting place of politicians and prime ministers, an attraction where both tourists and locals alike linger to see and be seen. But it's not for the fashion or the frivolity they gather here—it's for the food.

So how did it all start?

The word "brasserie" actually means "brewery" in French. In 1864, Frédéric Bofinger, a brewer from Alsace in northeastern France (the region that borders my own, Franche-Comté), made his way to Paris and opened a tiny bar in the heart of the Marais and Faubourg Saint-Antoine area. It served little more than draft beer and sauerkraut. At that time, numerous people were moving to Paris from war-torn Alsace in search of work, so there was a ready market. Beer on tap was unheard of in Paris back then and the quality of the sauerkraut was second to none. The combination took the city by storm and in no time brasseries were springing up all over Paris. The rest of France soon followed, and I think, for this reason, Bofinger could rightly claim to be the father of the Parisian brasserie. What started as a smoky bar filled with Alsatian refugees grew into a magnificent dining room with polished wood, gleaming brass and a stained-glass dome.

Today, brasseries are fashionable hotspots where politicians continue to rub shoulders with artists—but there is more to them than glamour. Brasseries are popular because the food they serve is homely, heart-warming and delicious. You can eat a simple sandwich or enjoy a *grand repas*, and they will often serve everything from early breakfasts right through to late suppers in the small hours. Among the famous brasseries in Paris are Bofinger, La Coupole and Brasserie Lipp, to name but a few. No matter where you are in France, however, if you find a good brasserie, you will find a good meal —and you won't have to pay a fortune for it either.

Some brasseries will be modern and chic and some laden with so much history they are practically national monuments. But choose carefully—there are plenty on main streets, but the best ones are often tucked away down side streets and hidden behind porchways.

How many restaurants can boast the illustrious likes of Ernest Hemingway, F. Scott Fitzgerald, Salvador Dalí, Henry

Miller, Pablo Picasso and Henri Matisse among their clientele? Well, La Coupole can. Few people take a trip to Paris without visiting this renowned brasserie at least once.

It is said, in 1944, when the Allied armies were poised to move into Paris to liberate it, the writer Ernest Hemingway became frustrated at the delay because he wanted to eat at his favorite brasserie. Borrowing a car, he drove unprotected into the French capital a whole day before the official liberators made their move and decided to "liberate" La Coupole personally. The things we do for the love of food!

From region to region

Brasseries make the most of local produce. There is a kind of regional pride, which guarantees you will always be served the best of whatever is grown or produced in the region. So eating in a brasserie in the South of France is a very different experience to eating in one in, say, Brittany. They all promote their own regional classics, often alongside well-known dishes from other areas. In Franche-Comté, my region, it can be Morteau sausage with sautéed potatoes and melted Vacherin Mont d'Or cheese. Up the road in Alsace, it can be *choucroute* (sauerkraut) or *baeckeoffe* (a kind of hotpot of potatoes, onion and pork). In Brest in Brittany, it can be sea bass baked in a sea-salt crust, and in Paris it might be *coq au vin*. And, if you are in one of France's great brasseries, you will probably find all these specialties on one menu. Whatever region you find yourself in, brasseries will always offer a great variety of food. So whether you want to have a quick meeting over a coffee and a croissant or to while away the hours with a friend over *steak frites* and a glass of red wine, you'll be in the right place.

Home from home

Actually, cooking French food doesn't need to be complicated, and bringing brasserie dishes into the home is returning them to their rightful place. After all, this is where most of them started, as most popular regional dishes served in brasseries will have been the ones that were originally firm family favorites. If you lived in Nancy, in Lorraine, for example, you would probably have eaten *quiche lorraine*; and if you lived in Bouches-du-Rhône, near Marseilles, it would have been *bouillabaisse* (a fish soup with saffron and tomatoes), *boudin noir* (blood sausage), *coq au vin, tarte aux pommes* (apple tart), *crème caramel*—all dishes cooked at home long before they were available in brasseries. Perhaps that's the reason why brasserie food has such a special place in our hearts.

The love of food has been with me as long as I can remember. My experience has come from sources that range from my grandmother to Michel Roux, but for me, the journey started with the wonderful home cooking of my grandmother. (I call her Grand-Mère in this book, although she was actually my great aunt; she took my natural grandmother's place so readily after her passing that it would have felt odd for us children to call her anything else.) My first memory is of Grand-Mère's kitchen on the small farm my grandparents owned in Franche-Comté, where I passed much of my childhood. I spent most Sunday afternoons and a large part of the summer vacations playing in haystacks around the farm with my brother and sister. If we weren't chasing cows, we were stealing cherries from the neighboring farm, stuffing as many as we could into our mouths and pockets before the farmer could catch us. Even now when I walk through fields, I find it hard to resist such temptations—old habits die hard, I guess!

If I close my eyes and think back, I can still recall the scent of freshly baked cakes luring me in from the fields. It wasn't long before I was in that kitchen constantly: watching, learning, helping Grand-Mère prepare the fruit I'd collected. I'm told, at the age of five, I stood in the middle of the kitchen and announced, "When I grow up, I'm going to be a chef!" Funny how history has a habit of repeating itself: I have a beautiful son who, strangely enough, at the age of five, stood in the middle of my kitchen and said, "When I grow up, I'm going to be a chef!" Well, what can you do?

My father, who was also called Daniel, played a large part, too. He was very close to nature, and walks were a daily routine he always said he couldn't do without. There was nothing he loved more—apart, perhaps, from hunting for food and then sharing the meal with family and friends. My father was what we call in France *une fine gueule*, which I can only translate as "somebody who really loves good food." We used to walk through the ancient, plentiful forests and he would tell me about the plants, the trees and the animal footprints we came across. I hold such special memories of those days.

Papa and I usually went pheasant hunting on a Saturday and so would be woken up on Sunday morning by the scent of delicately smoked bacon and pheasant roasting in red wine, which Maman (the other wonderful cook of my childhood) had been preparing since who knows what time. Sometimes there would even be an apple tart in the oven at the same time and the combination of aromas would drift up the stairs and pull us out of our cozy beds. The pheasant was normally prepared with braised cabbage and roasted turnips glazed in the pheasant *jus*. It was utterly delicious and quintessential French home cooking.

Maman was another great cook taught by Grand-Mère (she had no choice but to be a great cook because Papa loved food so much). I just happened to be around when she was cooking—eating, tasting and cooking—completely unaware my future was being shaped at that time.

When I became an apprentice chef at the age of fifteen, I had no idea how hard it was going to be. I had to complete three years before I could reach the next stage of becoming a commis chef, and there was still a long road ahead. I was catapulted from restaurant to restaurant, learning more and more as I went until, finally, I was given my first head chef position. Having reached this position, it started all over again. Passion, hard work and sheer bullheadedness somehow got me where I am today.

I hope my love of simple brasserie food not only encourages you to cook at home and enjoy the food you would normally just eat on vacation, but also inspires you to become hunters and gatherers again. How much more fun is it to take the children fruit picking or fishing than to drag them around the supermarket on a Saturday afternoon? I'm not expecting anyone to go out and spear the nearest wild boar, just to entice you to go, say, strawberry picking or foraging for wild garlic.

In this book, you will find some lovely, uncomplicated dishes that come from all over France. Some are traditional with a twist (for example, I have made them lighter or more up-to-date); others are specialties from particular regions but made my way. All of these recipes are ones that I cook at home with my wife, Claire, and son, Antoine. Hopefully, once you've tried them, you will make them again and again. I wanted to create a book that's not too "cheffy" (the kind that only chefs can follow), a straightforward home cookbook that's fun to read and inspires you to cook some really terrific French food—so don't leave it on the coffee table! If you use this cookbook on a regular basis, it will make me very happy.

A few technical terms

Here is a glossary of some of the culinary terms and techniques I've used when writing these recipes—you might be familiar with some of them, but less so others.

TO JULIENNE: Cut vegetables or fruit zest into thin sticks $\frac{1}{32}$ to $\frac{1}{16}$ inch thick and $1\frac{1}{4}$ inches long, using a knife or a mandoline. They are generally cooked in butter (and the zest in syrup), covered, until very soft. Raw vegetables that are to be served as an hors d'oeuvre can also be cut in juliennes.

TO BOIL: When using a deep saucepan with the amount of liquid required, you bring it to a boil over direct heat and maintain it for the specific time given in your recipe method.

TO POACH: When you cook food in a liquid (this can be water, bouillon, stock, or syrup) that is very hot but not bubbling, at a temperature just below the simmer. Suitable for gently cooking poultry, meat, vegetables, eggs or fruit, and delicate foods that could break in a vigorously bubbling liquid.

TO SIMMER: When you cook food in a hot liquid kept just below the boiling point and bubbling very gently.

TO BRAISE: When you roast or brown a piece of meat, poultry or vegetable in fat, then add a small amount of liquid and simmer in a covered pot over low heat.

TO FRY: To cook in hot fat (oil, butter or lard), with food either totally submerged (deep frying) or fat coming halfway up the food (pan-frying). Often used to cook vegetable juliennes, potatoes, fish and chicken.

TO GRILL: When you chargrill meat, poultry, fish or vegetables in a ridged grill pan over high heat, producing charred lines. These look impressive and create a lovely, subtle, caramelized flavor.

TO SAUTÉ: When you put a little fat (oil, butter or lard) in a shallow pan, add potatoes, vegetables, mushrooms, meat, poultry or fruits and quickly toss them to brown or cook through. It is important to keep the food moving around the pan while you are sautéeing.

TO DEGLAZE: When, after sautéeing, you add a liquid, such as alcohol, juice or vinegar, stir to dissolve the caramelized brown bits in the pan, and then allow half to evaporate quickly. If you are using alcohol, you can set it alight (*flamber* it).

TO REDUCE: When you have a lot of liquid in a pan, and you need to decrease the volume over medium to high heat. Make sure you get to the level or consistency directed in the recipe method.

CONFIT: When a piece of pork, goose, duck or turkey is cooked in its own fat and stored in a pot, it is called *confit*. A vegetable confit will be made with olive oil. To "confit" something is one of the oldest means of storing food.

RAGOUT: A stew made from meat, poultry, game, fish or vegetables cut into uniform-size and -shape pieces and cooked with or without first being browned in a sauté pan. It is generally flavored with herbs and spices. The ragout dates back to the seventeenth century when, in classic French, the word was used to describe anything that stimulated the appetite.

TIAN: The name given to a dish that consists of alternate layers of sliced vegetables. It might be made with or without onions and garlic, but will definitely be sprinkled with herbs and well seasoned. It is also the name of Provençal earthenware pots traditionally used to cook the dish in.

Mayonnaise au safran

Pâte à tarte Grand-Mère

Fond d'agneau

Vinaigrette

Pâte brisée

Crème pâtissière

Pâte sucrée

Pâte à choux

Pâte à crêpes

Les Bases
THE BASICS

Stocks, sauces and pastry dough are essential ingredients in many classic French dishes, and in this chapter I will be showing you how to make them. With my stocks, I like to have the real flavor of the main ingredient coming through —the intensity is the vital thing. Sauces are important, too. Although they are often made with a few, simple ingredients, they can transform a plain dish into something really special. I'm passionate about good pastry, which is the foundation of many of my favorite recipes and essential to a good pie or tart—whether it's savory or sweet.

Fond de volaille

CHICKEN STOCK

Makes about 2 quarts
Preparation time 10 minutes, plus
* 1 hour cooling*
Cooking time 2 hours 40 minutes

4½ pounds chicken wings or bones,
   or 2 chicken carcasses

1 thyme sprig

2 carrots, peeled and halved
   lengthwise

1 small handful of curly parsley
   stems

1 small onion, unpeeled and halved

6 black peppercorns

Put all the ingredients in a large, heavy-bottomed saucepan, cover with 4 quarts cold water and bring to a boil over high heat. As soon as the stock starts to boil, foam will begin to form on the surface. Reduce the heat to low and skim off the foam, using a ladle, then simmer gently, uncovered, 2 to 2½ hours. By this time the liquid will reduce by half and the flavor will intensify. Remove the pan from the heat, pass the stock through a strainer, using a ladle to help you, then leave it to cool at least 1 hour. Your stock is now ready to use.

If you want to freeze your stock, divide the cool stock into small plastic tubs with lids, leaving some space for it to expand, and pop the containers in the freezer. Your stock will keep up to 4 weeks.

Fond d'agneau

LAMB STOCK

Makes about 2 quarts
Preparation time 15 minutes, plus
* 1 hour cooling*
Cooking time 3 hours 50 minutes

2¾ pounds lamb bones, well
   trimmed

2 tablespoons olive oil

1 rosemary or thyme sprig

2 parsley sprigs

1 garlic bulb, unpeeled and halved
   crosswise

1 small onion, unpeeled and
   quartered

6 black peppercorns

2 large tomatoes, quartered

Heat the oven to 350°F. Put the bones in a roasting pan and roast 20 minutes, or until golden brown, stirring occasionally to make sure they color evenly. Remove the bones from the pan and put them in a large, heavy-bottomed saucepan. Add all the remaining ingredients, except the tomatoes, and cook over medium heat 10 minutes. Add the tomatoes, then cook 10 minutes longer.

Add 4 quarts cold water and bring to a boil over high heat. As soon as the stock starts to boil, foam will begin to form on the surface. Reduce the heat to low and skim off the foam, using a ladle. Simmer 1 hour, uncovered, then top up the water to its previous level and simmer 2 hours longer. By this time the liquid will reduce by half. Remove the pan from the heat, pass the stock through a strainer, using a ladle to help you, then leave it to cool at least 1 hour. The stock should be a lovely, shiny, clear, golden brown color. It is now ready to use.

If you want to freeze your stock, divide the cool stock into small plastic tubs with lids, leaving some space for it to expand, and pop the containers in the freezer. Your stock will keep up to 4 weeks.

Fumet de poisson

FISH STOCK

Makes about 2 quarts
Preparation time 10 minutes, plus
   1 hour cooling
Cooking time 2 hours 40 minutes

2¾ pounds fresh fish bones, flesh
   removed

1 small handful of curly parsley
   stems

1 small onion, unpeeled and
   quartered

1 thyme sprig

1 celery stick, peeled and halved

6 black peppercorns

Place the fish bones in a large bowl, cover with cold water and leave to rest 10 minutes, then rinse thoroughly using a strainer. Repeat 3 times.

Put the bones in a large, heavy-bottomed saucepan with all the other ingredients, cover with 4 quarts cold water and bring to a boil over high heat. As soon as the stock starts to boil, foam will begin to form on the surface. Reduce the heat to low and skim off the foam, using a ladle, then simmer gently, uncovered, 2 to 2¹/₂ hours. By this time the liquid will reduce by half and the flavor will intensify. Remove the pan from the heat, pass the stock through a strainer, using a ladle to help you, then leave it to cool at least 1 hour. Your stock is now ready to use.

If you want to freeze your stock, divide the cooled stock into small plastic tubs with lids, leaving some space for it to expand, and pop the containers in the freezer. Your stock will keep for up to 4 weeks.

Bouillon de légumes

VEGETABLE STOCK

Makes about 1¹/₂ quarts
Preparation time 15 minutes, plus
   1 hour cooling
Cooking time 2 hours 15 minutes

2 tablespoons olive oil

1 celery stick, peeled and chopped,
   or 1 small handful of celery leaves

1 thyme sprig

1 scallion, chopped

1 handful of parsley stems, chopped

1 garlic clove

2 carrots, peeled and halved
   lengthwise

2 new potatoes, halved

6 black peppercorns

2 button mushrooms, halved

Briefly warm the oil in a large saucepan over medium heat. Add all the remaining ingredients and cook, partially covered, 10 minutes. Add 3 quarts cold water and bring to a boil over high heat, then reduce the heat to low and simmer, uncovered, 2 hours, or until reduced by half. Remove the pan from the heat and pass the stock through a strainer, using a ladle to help you, then leave it to cool at least 1 hour. Your stock is now ready to use.

If you want to freeze your stock, divide the cooled stock into small plastic tubs with lids, leaving some space for it to expand, and pop the containers in the freezer. Your stock will keep up to 4 weeks.

Vinaigrette

FRENCH VINAIGRETTE

Makes ¾ cup
Preparation time 5 minutes

2 teaspoons Dijon mustard

2 tablespoons red or white wine vinegar or balsamic vinegar

½ cup olive oil or canola oil

sea salt and freshly ground black pepper

In a small bowl or pitcher, whisk together the mustard, vinegar and 2 tablespoons water, then whisk in the oil. You should have a thick, glossy liquid. Season with salt and pepper.

Use straightaway or cover and keep in the refrigerator up to 1 week.

Sauce hollandaise

HOLLANDAISE SAUCE

Makes about 1¾ cups
Preparation time 5 minutes
Cooking time 25 minutes

2 tablespoons white wine vinegar

2 extra-large egg yolks, beaten

1½ cups butter, melted

juice of ½ lemon

sea salt and freshly ground black pepper

Put 6 tablespoons water in a small saucepan over medium heat. Add the vinegar, season with salt and pepper and simmer 2 minutes, or until it reduces by half and the liquid becomes syrupy. Transfer the vinegar reduction to a heatproof bowl and rest it over a saucepan of simmering water, making sure the bottom of the bowl does not touch the water (this is called a bain-marie). Add the egg yolks and beat the mixture continuously over low heat until it turns white, thickens and the liquid coats the back of a spoon. Don't let the water boil or your sauce will be scrambled eggs!

Now add the melted butter to the vinegar reduction a little at a time, omitting any "milk solids" that form at the bottom of the pan, whisking continuously. When it starts to thicken, add 1 tablespoon water, then continue adding the butter until it is all incorporated. The mixture should be smooth and light—you might need to add a little more water to achieve this consistency. Season again with salt and pepper and keep warm in the bain-marie until ready to serve. Just before serving, squeeze in a few drops of lemon juice. Taste and add more juice if you like a stronger lemon flavor.

Mayonnaise au safran

SAFFRON MAYONNAISE

Makes ¾ cup plus 2 tablespoons
Preparation time 10 minutes
Cooking time 5 minutes

a good pinch of saffron threads

2 egg yolks

1 tablespoon French mustard

⅔ cup sunflower or grapeseed oil

1 garlic clove, finely chopped

a squeeze of lemon juice (optional)

sea salt and freshly ground black
   pepper

To create your essence of saffron, put the saffron and 2 tablespoons water in a small saucepan over low heat. Simmer 4 to 5 minutes to let the saffron release its flavor and color. When it is a strong, deep-orange color, strain the liquid into a bowl and, using a whisk, beat the egg yolks and mustard into it. Season with salt and pepper and a few drops of lemon, if liked, then drizzle in the oil, a little at a time, stirring continuously. Add the garlic and then whisk in 2 tablespoons hot water to help it bind. The mayonnaise should be glossy and luscious!

Keep in the refrigerator and serve cold.

Sauce vierge

SAUCE VIERGE

Makes 1⅔ cups
Preparation time 10 minutes
Cooking time 3 minutes

4 tablespoons extra virgin olive oil

1 shallot, chopped

1 tomato, seeded and diced

juice of ½ lime

1 tablespoon balsamic vinegar

1 handful of flat-leaf parsley, finely
   chopped

sea salt and freshly ground black
   pepper

Put the oil in a small saucepan and briefly warm it over low heat about 30 seconds. Add the shallot and cook 2 minutes. Remove the pan from the heat and stir in the tomato, lime juice and balsamic vinegar. Just before serving, add the parsley and season with salt and pepper. Enjoy warm drizzled over your dish.

Baking was Grand-Mère Suzanne's thing, and most of the time, she did it without measuring. She knew whether something was right just by looking at it, and when it came to cakes and tarts, no one could match her. Grand-Mère's pastry is sweet, and is great for apple, pear and mixed-fruit tarts—actually it's great for all desserts in general.

Pâte à tarte de Grand-Mère

GRAND-MÈRE'S SWEET PASTRY DOUGH

Makes enough for an 11-inch tart pan
Preparation time 15 minutes, plus
* 30 minutes chilling*

½ cup unsalted butter, roughly
   diced and softened to room
   temperature

⅔ cup confectioners' sugar, sifted,
   plus extra for dusting

1 egg

2 egg yolks

2 cups all-purpose flour, plus extra
   for kneading the dough

Put the butter and sugar in a large mixing bowl and beat with a wooden spoon until nice and creamy. Stir in the egg and egg yolks, then add the flour and mix everything together with your fingers until it forms a lovely crumbly texture. Press the mixture together to form a ball.

On a lightly-floured surface, knead the dough with the palm of your hand 1 to 2 minutes until it forms a ball easily and is soft to the touch. Watch out—don't overwork the dough or it will go back to the crumbly texture! Flatten it slightly with the palm of your hand, wrap it in plastic wrap and leave in the refrigerator at least 30 minutes before use. This helps it to relax—and, meanwhile, so can you!

Pâte sucrée

SWEET PIECRUST DOUGH

Makes enough for an 11-inch tart pan
Preparation time 15 minutes, plus
* 2 hours chilling*

¾ cup butter, at room temperature

a pinch of salt

1 tablespoon superfine sugar

1 egg yolk

3 tablespoons milk or water, at room
   temperature

2 cups all-purpose flour

Put the butter, salt, sugar, egg yolk and milk in a mixing bowl and mix together by hand. Add the flour slowly, mixing until just combined.

Be careful not to overwork it or it will become too elastic. When the dough is ready, either wrap it in a clean cotton dish towel or put it on a plate and cover with a clean cotton dish towel, then leave in the refrigerator at least 2 hours before using—this relaxes the dough and makes it easier to use.

Pâte brisée
SAVORY PIECRUST DOUGH

Makes enough for an 11-inch tart pan
Preparation time 15 minutes, plus
2 hours chilling

½ cup butter, roughly diced and
softened to room temperature

2 cups all-purpose flour, plus extra
for kneading the dough

a pinch of salt

1 egg yolk

3 tablespoons milk or water

Put the butter, flour and salt in a mixing bowl and mix together by hand until it is a crumbly, powdery texture. Add the egg yolk and milk and continue working the dough until the ingredients are combined and the texture is smooth. On a lightly floured surface, knead the dough 1 to 2 minutes until silky smooth. When the dough is ready, either wrap it in a clean cotton dish towel or put it on a plate and cover with a clean cotton dish towel, then leave it in the refrigerator at least 2 hours before using—this relaxes the dough and makes it easier to use.

Pâte à choux
CHOUX PASTRY DOUGH

Makes 30 to 40 profiteroles
Preparation time 15 minutes, plus
40 minutes resting and making the
crème pâtissière
Cooking time 40 minutes

¾ cup plus 1 teaspoon butter

1 teaspoon salt

scant 1 tablespoon sugar

2 cups all-purpose flour

8 eggs

a few drops of vanilla extract

Crème Pâtissière (see page 24) or
extra-thick custard sauce flavored
with chocolate, vanilla or crushed
hazelnuts, if liked, for filling

Put the butter, salt, sugar and 2 cups water in a large saucepan and bring to a boil. Remove the pan from the heat, add the flour and mix to combine, using a whisk. Return the pan to medium heat and stir gently with a wooden spoon until the mixture starts to dry and comes off the spoon easily and "sweats" slightly. Remove the pan from the heat again and add the eggs, one by one, whisking gently, until they are totally absorbed by the paste. You should have a lovely yellow, silky mixture. Stir in the vanilla extract and set the dough aside to rest 35 to 40 minutes.

Heat the oven to 365°F and line a baking sheet with parchment paper. Using a pastry bag, pipe the dough onto the baking sheet to make 1-inch-thick balls. Bake 20 minutes, then turn the oven off and leave the profiteroles inside 10 minutes longer for them to dry. They should be very light. Remove the baking sheet from the oven, then transfer the profiteroles to a cooling rack and leave to cool completely.

To fill the profiteroles, cut open from the bottom to the top, using a sharp knife, and pipe in the filling of your choice, such as Crème Pâtissière or extra-thick flavored custard sauce.

Crème anglaise

VANILLA CUSTARD SAUCE

Makes scant 1½ quarts
Preparation time 30 minutes
Cooking time 25 minutes

4¼ cups plus 2 tablespoons whole
  milk

1 vanilla bean, halved lengthwise

8 egg yolks

¾ cup sugar

Put the milk in a medium saucepan over low heat. Scrape the vanilla seeds into the milk, using a knife. Whisk, then throw in the vanilla bean as well. Simmer at least 15 minutes to get the maximum flavor out of the seeds. Meanwhile, whisk the egg yolks and sugar together in a large bowl.

Add the egg-yolk mixture to the milk and cook over medium heat 5 to 8 minutes, stirring continuously (otherwise you will get scrambled eggs!) until it starts to thicken. You will be able to tell when it's ready if when you run 2 fingers down the back of the spoon the two lines don't immediately join. (If the custard does start to scramble, don't panic—you can rescue it by pouring the mixture into a food processor, removing the vanilla bean and blending until it regains a smooth, thick texture.) Strain immediately into a clean bowl and stir for a few minutes to cool the mixture down, then put it in the refrigerator to chill.

⚫━━━━━━►◦◦◦◦◦━━━━━━

Crème pâtissière

CRÈME PÂTISSIÈRE

Makes 3¼ cups
Preparation time 15 minutes
Cooking time 10 to 15 minutes

2 cups plus 2 tablespoons whole
  milk

1 vanilla bean, halved lengthwise

5 egg yolks

½ cup superfine sugar

scant ⅓ cup cornstarch

small knob of butter

Put the milk in a medium saucepan over low heat. Scrape the vanilla seeds into the milk, using a knife. Whisk, then throw in the vanilla bean as well. Heat the milk until it is almost simmering, remove the pan from the heat and leave to infuse about 20 minutes. Remove the vanilla bean from the milk and clean and dry with paper towels—you can use it again.

Meanwhile, whisk the egg yolks with the sugar in a bowl until the mixture is light, thick and creamy and the sugar dissolves. Gradually add the cornstarch, a spoonful at a time, whisking well after each addition to avoid lumps. Slowly pour half the infused milk into the egg mixture, beating the mixture as you pour, then transfer the mixture back into the saucepan with the remaining milk. Place over medium-low heat and stir continuously and quickly 10 minutes, or until the mixture begins to thicken. Remove the pan from the heat and continue to stir until the mixture cools and is lovely and smooth, thick and slightly trembling.

Pour into a container and rub with a small piece of butter—just enough to cover the top to avoid the surface drying out and forming a crust. Set aside until required. This is ideal for the Summer Fruit Tart on page 185.

Pâte à crêpes

BASIC CREPES

Makes 12 to 15 crepes
Preparation time 10 minutes
Cooking time 45 minutes

1 cup all-purpose flour

2 tablespoons sugar

a few drops of vanilla extract

a pinch of salt

2 eggs

1¼ cups milk (whole or 2%)

2 tablespoons butter, melted, plus
    extra for frying, if needed

lemon juice and sugar, to serve

Put the flour, sugar, vanilla extract, salt, eggs and scant 1/2 cup of the milk in a bowl. Add the butter and whisk until smooth, then whisk in the remaining milk. Alternatively, if it's easier for you, just pop everything into a blender and blend for a few minutes, then slowly add the remaining milk and blend a little more. The important thing is to make sure there are not any lumps and the consistency is runny, so your crepes will be thin and light. When you make the batter gradually like this, there is no need to set it aside to rest.

Heat a 6- to 7-inch nonstick crepe pan or skillet over medium-high heat. If you use a nonstick pan, you won't have to add butter to the pan as there is some already in the batter, although extra butter can make the flipping easier. If you're not using a nonstick pan, add a little butter to the pan first to keep the crepes from sticking.

Using a ladle, pour enough batter into the pan to cover the bottom thinly. Swirl the pan around to help spread the batter, if necessary, then cook 1 to 1 1/2 minutes. Now comes the fun part—try to flip it, or you can use a spatula to turn it over. Cook 1 to 2 minutes longer on the second side.

Remove the crepe from the pan and repeat with the remaining batter, adding more butter to the pan, if necessary.

Sprinkle the crepes with lemon juice and sugar, or any other topping you like, such as jam or jelly, marmalade or ice cream. Enjoy!

Soupe de petits pois aux lardons

Caviar d'aubergine

Tapenade

Soupe à l'oignon gratinée au comté

Tomates séchées au four

Soupe de poisson avec mayonnaise au safran

Croque Monsieur au jambon et comté

Les Entrées
APPETIZERS

Appetizers are an important part of a meal in France, but they differ hugely from region to region. The recipes I've chosen here are specialties from all over the country. There is Duck Rillettes from the Dordogne, Fish Soup with Saffron Mayonnaise from the coastal regions and a selection of Tapenade and Eggplant Caviar from Provence, perhaps served with some cheese, charcuterie and crusty bread. With a glass of wine and good company, each of these first courses is a tantalizing treat to take you on to your dinner.

Soothing, velvety and rich, leek and potato soup is the ultimate comforting winter soup. If you want it to be very green, use small leeks and make sure you use the green part—lots of people throw this away thinking it is no good, but that is actually where the goodness and color lie. To get rid of the grit and soil caught between layers, cut the leek into quarters, lengthwise from just above the root to the top, but don't cut through the root. Fan out the layers and swirl them around in a bowl of water.

Soupe de poireaux et pommes de terre aux champignons sauvages

LEEK & POTATO SOUP WITH WILD MUSHROOMS

Preparation time 20 minutes, plus making the stock
Cooking time 30 minutes

3 tablespoons butter

2 medium or 5 small leeks, chopped and rinsed, keeping the white and green parts separate

2 large potatoes, peeled and diced

1 garlic clove, chopped

1 thyme sprig

1 shallot, peeled and chopped

2 cups plus 2 tablespoons Vegetable Stock (see page 19) or Chicken Stock (see page 18)

4 tablespoons crème fraîche, plus extra to serve

1 heaping cup sliced wild or button mushrooms

1 tablespoon snipped chives

sea salt and freshly ground black pepper

toasted baguette or farmhouse bread, to serve

Melt 2 tablespoons of the butter slowly in a large, heavy-bottomed saucepan over medium heat. Add the white part of the leeks and the potatoes, garlic, thyme and shallot and cook, partially covered, 4 to 5 minutes. Stir occasionally, taking care not to let them color. Add the stock and 1 cup water and season with salt. Bring to a boil, then reduce the heat to low and simmer 15 to 20 minutes until the potatoes are soft. Remove the thyme sprig.

Shortly before the potatoes finish cooking, bring a medium saucepan of salted water to a boil. Add the green part of the leeks to the boiling water and blanch 3 to 4 minutes, then drain, pour ice-cold water over hem to seal in the color and drain again. For maximum color and a strong, earthy flavor, blanch the leeks just before blending with the potatoes. Transfer the blanched green leeks and the potato and leek mixture to a blender, season with salt and pepper and blend until very smooth, then add the crème fraîche. You might have to do this in batches, depending on the size of your blender. Pour the soup into a clean saucepan (passing it through a strainer if you want it really smooth) and keep warm over low heat while you prepare the mushrooms.

Melt the remaining butter in a nonstick skillet over medium heat. When it is foaming, add the mushrooms, season with salt and pepper and cook, stirring occasionally, 2 minutes, or until golden brown. Remove the pan from the heat and throw in the chives.

Put a spoonful of mushrooms in each bowl, pour the leek soup over them and top with a swirl of crème fraîche. Serve with bread. Creamy, simple and satisfying.

Wild garlic has a short season—about six weeks at the most—starting in early spring. You will find it in woodlands and alongside streams or canals, but if you can't go looking for it yourself, try your local farmers' markets. The smell is strong and distinctly garlicky, and the leaves look somewhat like spinach, only paler, and it is this combination that makes this a wonderfully tasty soup. The white flowers are also great in salads. When wild garlic is not in season, make this soup using spinach instead.

Soupe d'ail sauvage

WILD GARLIC SOUP

Preparation time 15 minutes, plus
making the stock
Cooking time 25 minutes

2 tablespoons butter

1 small onion, chopped

1 large potato, peeled and chopped

3½ cups Vegetable Stock (see page 19) or Chicken Stock (see page 18)

1 pound 5 ounces wild garlic leaves

4 tablespoons crème fraîche, or to taste, plus extra to serve

sea salt and freshly ground black pepper

Melt the butter in a medium saucepan over low heat. Add the onion and cook 4 to 5 minutes, stirring occasionally, until soft and pale without color. Add the potato, season with salt and cook 3 to 4 minutes, stirring so it does not stick to the bottom of the pan.

Add the stock and bring to a boil over high heat, then reduce the heat to low and simmer 10 minutes, or until the potato is soft. Add the wild garlic leaves and cook 5 minutes longer. You want to keep the color, so don't overcook.

Transfer the soup to a blender and blend until smooth. You might have to do this in batches, depending on the size of your blender. Add the crème fraîche, according to your taste, and season with salt and pepper. Serve warm, topped with an extra swirl of crème fraîche.

During the spring months, peas are one of my favorite vegetables. They seem underused in general, which is a pity because when cooked well they are so sweet and crunchy. Pea shoots add more depth of color and flavor to this soup. They can be difficult to find, although you might find them at farmers' markets or good supermarkets—it will definitely be worth your trouble. The freshness of peas combined with the rich saltiness of pancetta makes this a soup with style and substance.

Soupe de petits pois aux lardons

PEA & PANCETTA SOUP

Preparation time 20 minutes, plus making the stock
Cooking time 35 minutes

2 tablespoons butter

1 small leek, halved lengthwise, rinsed and sliced

1 small potato, peeled and thinly sliced

4½ to 5 cups Chicken Stock (see page 18) or Vegetable Stock (see page 19)

3½ cups shelled fresh or frozen peas

2 ounces pea shoots (optional), plus extra to serve

4 tablespoons heavy cream, plus extra to serve

3 ounces pancetta, cut into strips

sea salt and freshly ground black pepper

farmhouse bread, to serve

Melt the butter in a medium saucepan over low heat. Add the leek and potato and cook, stirring occasionally, 5 minutes. Add the chicken stock and bring to a boil over high heat, adjusting the amount of stock you add according to whether you like a thicker or thinner soup. Reduce the heat to low again and simmer 10 to 12 minutes until the potato is soft. Turn the heat down to its lowest setting and add the peas and pea shoots, if using. Simmer slowly 5 minutes.

Transfer the mixture to a blender, season with salt and pepper and blend to the desired texture, adding the cream at the end. You might have to do this in batches, depending on the size of your blender. Pour the soup into a clean pan (passing it through a strainer if you want it really smooth) and keep warm over low heat while you prepare the pancetta.

Bring a small saucepan of water to a boil. Add the pancetta, return the water to a boil and then remove the pan from the heat. This will remove excess fat and salt. Drain the pancetta and pat it dry on paper towels. Heat a nonstick skillet over medium heat, add the pancetta and fry 4 to 5 minutes, tossing until crisp.

Put a spoonful of pancetta in each bowl and pour the soup over. Add a swirl of cream and a sprig of pea shoots, if using, and serve with bread. This is a lovely spring soup.

During spring and summer, wild watercress can be found in abundance alongside streams and rivers. Young watercress leaves are softer and less bitter than the older ones, so try to get these if you can. This soup has a deep, herb-green color and a delicate, grassy flavor, and it is full of goodness. The key to keeping the color is to cook it very gently and for a short time. The finished result should be smooth in texture, rich in color and peppery in taste. For an extra-special touch, serve with a poached quail egg on a slice of toasted baguette.

Soupe de cresson de fontaine et pommes de terre, oeuf de caille sur croûtons

WATERCRESS & POTATO SOUP WITH QUAIL EGG CROUTONS

Preparation time 25 minutes
Cooking time 30 minutes

2 tablespoons butter

2 shallots, chopped

1 large leek, sliced and rinsed

2 cups peeled and diced potatoes

10 ounces watercress sprigs, stems removed

4 tablespoons heavy cream, plus extra to serve

1 baguette

1 teaspoon vinegar

4 quail eggs

sea salt and ground white pepper

Melt the butter in a medium saucepan over low heat. Add the shallots and leek and cook, stirring occasionally, 3 to 4 minutes, then add the potatoes and enough boiling water to cover generously, about 3 cups. Simmer 10 to 12 minutes until the potatoes are soft. Remove the pan from the heat, add the watercress, cover and set aside 4 to 5 minutes.

Transfer the mixture to a blender, season with salt and pepper and blend until smooth, adding the cream at the end. Don't be shy with the seasoning, as watercress can take quite a lot. If you like your soup with a finer texture, pass it through a strainer into a clean saucepan and warm through—very gently or the chlorophyll will break down and the soup will lose its fabulous, vibrant color.

Toast 4 slices of baguette. Bring a small saucepan of water to a gentle simmer, then add the vinegar. Carefully break the quail eggs, one at a time, into the water and poach 1 to 2 minutes—the egg yolks should remain soft. Remove the eggs using a slotted spoon and rest the spoon on paper towels. Carefully pat dry the eggs. Put a warm, toasted bread slice in each bowl, top each with a poached egg and pierce the eggs so the yolks run down into the soup bowls. Pour the soup into each bowl around the baguette slice, add a swirl of cream and serve with the remaining baguette on the side.

Like the sea itself, this soup is powerful and aromatic. When I eat it, it makes me think of standing on a high rock, breathing in the salty sea air. Fish soups are found in brasseries in coastal villages and cities from Marseille to Bordeaux to Brest. They differ according not only to the variety of fish used but also where they are caught—fish from warm water have a different flavor from fish from cold water, for example. In France, the type of fish used will be typical to the area and most likely true to a recipe that has been passed down from generation to generation or from chef to chef. Either way, everyone will claim theirs is best!

Soupe de poisson avec mayonnaise au safran

FISH SOUP WITH SAFFRON MAYONNAISE

Preparation time 20 minutes, plus making the mayonnaise
Cooking time 1 hour 10 minutes

4 tablespoons olive oil

4 garlic cloves, crushed

1 fennel bulb, chopped

2 onions, sliced

4 small soft shell crabs (optional)

1¾ pounds mixed fish, such as monkfish, porgy, croaker, ocean perch and goatfish or rouget, drawn and dressed as required (you can ask your fish merchant to do this)

4 tablespoons aniseed liqueur, such as Pastis or Pernod

1 heaping cup chopped tomatoes

4 tablespoons tomato paste

1 bay leaf

a pinch of saffron powder

a pinch of cayenne pepper

sea salt and freshly ground black pepper

croutons, to serve

½ recipe quantity Saffron Mayonnaise (see page 21), to serve

Warm the oil in a large, deep skillet or cast-iron pan over medium heat. Add the garlic, fennel and onions and cook, stirring often to avoid discoloring, 3 to 5 minutes until soft.

Add the crabs, if using, and cook 4 to 5 minutes until the shells become red. Add the fish and cook over medium-high heat 5 minutes longer, stirring to make sure it doesn't stick to the bottom. Add the Pastis, tomatoes, tomato paste, bay leaf, saffron, cayenne pepper and 2 quarts water. Bring to a boil, then reduce the heat to medium and simmer 50 minutes. After that time, the flesh should come away from the fish bones. Remove and discard the bones.

Transfer the soup to a blender and blend until smooth. It will be a little thick, but that is exactly how you want it. Pass it through a strainer, if desired, into a clean saucepan, reheat and season with salt and pepper.

Serve with croutons and saffron mayonnaise.

This soup is at the heart of French cooking. It is made in homes and brasseries right across France and loved by all. You will need some really good onions, like the white ones from Provence or your local farmer's supply. Being from Franche-Comté, I think this dish tastes best when the croutons are made with the famous Comté cheese. The combination of rich, golden cheese melting into the tangy, glistening onions makes it second to none. This is a great soup to have on the stovetop to share with friends after a night out on the town.

Soupe à l'oignon gratinée au comté
ONION SOUP WITH COMTÉ CHEESE CROUTONS

Preparation time 30 minutes
Cooking time 45 minutes

6 tablespoons butter

6 onions, sliced

2 tablespoons all-purpose flour

4 tablespoons red wine

scant ½ cup white wine

1 teaspoon sugar (optional)

4 thick slices baguette

2 tablespoons olive oil

1 cup grated Comté cheese

sea salt and freshly ground black
   pepper

Melt the butter in a large saucepan over low heat. Add the onions, season with salt and pepper and cook, partially covered, 10 minutes, or until they are a golden color. Stir often so they don't burn. Sprinkle with the flour and cook 10 minutes longer, or until the onions start to brown.

In a large heatproof container, mix together the wines and 7 cups boiling water, then slowly pour the mixture over the onions, stirring continuously to prevent lumps. Bring to a boil over high heat, skimming away any impurities from the surface, then reduce the heat to low and simmer 15 to 20 minutes. Taste the soup and adjust the salt and pepper. If it seems too sour, add a little sugar to taste.

Meanwhile, to make the cheese croutons, heat the broiler to high. Put the baguette slices on a baking sheet, drizzle with the olive oil and sprinkle with the grated cheese. Broil 4 to 5 minutes until the cheese melts, bubbles and is golden brown, being careful not to burn the edges of the croutons.

Divide the soup into bowls, pop the croutons on top and enjoy. If it is less than heavenly, I want to know why!

CHEF'S TIP: *The traditional way to make this soup is with water, as I've done here. If you want a richer soup, however, you can replace the water with either vegetable or chicken stock. You could also serve it with garlic croutons, if liked. Instead of melting cheese on the baguette, drizzle the slices with olive oil, lightly toast them under the broiler and then rub with garlic cloves that you've cut in half to release maximum flavor.*

Les Pains

Breads

For me, bread has always been significant not only because I love it, but also because it goes so well with so many other foods, such as cheese, pâté, charcuterie, hot and cold meats and much more.

Bread is close to a religion in France. All over the country bakeries (*boulangeries*) take turns so there is always one open every day of the week. On Saturdays and Sundays they are open all day. The best-known French bread of all, the classic baguette (meaning "stick" in French) is the only bread to be sold at a fixed price across France because the government considers it essential to life! New batches appear on shelves all day long because it should always be eaten fresh, and can become chewy very quickly. You often see people on trains or riding bikes with a baguette under their arm.

The breaking of bread is a great gesture that has no equal around the table, one that creates a sense of sharing and friendship, whether it's a simple baguette or *boule* (round-shaped, generally white bread, available in different sizes and types of flours), a *pain de campagne* (a rustic loaf with a thick crust and one of the most popular farmhouse breads) or more exotic types such as *pain aux noix* (bread made with nuts), *pain aux raisins* (bread made with raisins) or *fougasse* (a focaccia-type bread, very popular in the South of France).

Most traditional versions of *pain de campagne* are made with a mixture of white, wholewheat and/ or rye flour, water, leavening and salt. When sliced diagonally and served with charcuterie and gherkins, there's nothing better. *Pain aux noix* is delicious with foie gras and both *pain aux noix* and *pain aux raisins* go extremely well with cheese. *Fougasse* is often made with bacon (*aux lardons*), onions (*aux oignons*), herbs (*aux herbes*), olives (*aux olives*) or anchovies (*aux anchois*). You probably wouldn't set out to buy these breads, but when you see them on display, you can't resist them! Before you know it you have bought the cheese to go with them, and maybe some wine, too, and you have a perfect impromptu meal!

In France, it seems everyone has their own favorite baker. In small villages and in towns like mine the *boulangerie* is always a rendez-vous for locals, where they can chat about anything and everything and usually, by the time they've finished, they realize they've finished the baguette, too, so they have to go back to buy another one!

As a child, I often used to do the shopping. When I was very young and not that tall, I could not reach the counter in some shops, so I would just hand over the note Maman had written for me and be given whatever food we were having that day for lunch or dinner. My last shop was always the baker, where I'd pick up one or two baguettes and one "long bread" (a longer version of the baguette).

Another popular baguette variation is the *ficelle* (French for "string" because it is thin), which is generally used for quick snacks. As children we used to love to put a bar of dark chocolate in our *ficelle* for our *quatre heures*, our after-school snack. We also enjoyed *pain de mie*, a soft, semisweet loaf with a thin crust, mainly used for sandwiches; *pain au lait*, a sweet roll that is very moist and easy to eat because it doesn't have a crust, and *pain de seigle*, made from two-thirds rye flour, one-third wheat flour, a tasty alternative to baguette, and great with cheese or charcuterie.

On the way home from shopping trips, I'd start eating one of the baguettes, sometimes devouring more than half. It was still warm and tasted so good that I simply could not resist it. The smell used to tempt me so much, just as it did when I entered the bakery right after bread had been baked, or *croissants* and *pains au chocolat* had just come out of the oven. It is those moments I cannot forget and which I love to experience again when I go back home. It's wonderful to hold the bread to your ear and slowly crush it so that it crackles at the same time that it releases its warm, just-baked aroma! How could I ever *not* eat bread?

But real bread is in danger. Mass-produced bread is in demand. Quickly made with fast-growing crops, such bread is often too heavy, very poor in natural nutrients and filled with yeast substitutes. Simple, good, healthy bread, made naturally, is what we should be eating. Long live the traditional bakers, masters of their trade, passionate about their art, working all night to guarantee their faithful clients remain the same and spread the word.

I have always considered the art of baking, along with the other culinary arts, to be a very noble profession, where you create wonderful food with your own hands. In this book, you will find recipes where bread is central and other ingredients complement it, not the other way around. There are the delicious Croque Monsieur and Croque Madame, made from day-old bread, toasted farmhouse bread with *rillettes* or croutons in onion soup, and many more. Always buy good bread to serve with your meals and don't compromise on ingredients. Find a good baker and freeze the loaves so you can always enjoy tasty bread. Or, if you make your own, use a reputable flour, organic if possible (or, even better, stoneground), and buy high quality, not bleached. Then, using good yeast, you will get a great result that is much healthier for your family.

A BRIEF HISTORY OF BREAD

Humans have been making bread for at least 8,000 years, but it wasn't always good to eat. Early, unleavened versions were cooked on a slate stone, which made the bread so tough you could lose your teeth eating it! A 4,000-year-old sample on display at London's British Museum is proof of how far the craft of bread-baking has come.

Legend has it we owe our modern-day bread to a young Egyptian, who once forgot to cook his dough. After a while, it began to ferment and the yeast cultures that are naturally found in flour became active. When he eventually did cook it, the dough rose, becoming the first leavened bread. Today, artisan bakers in France often produce their own yeast for leavened bread by preparing a "growth culture," which they constantly refresh, so it provides leavening for years. It gives the bread a special flavor and texture. This *pain au levain* (traditionally leavened bread) is generally bought as a massive *boule* (ball), cut into long slices and served with butter.

The Egyptians were expert wheat growers, and sold their excess crop to the Greeks, who went on to develop the bread-making technique farther. The Romans then learned from them. They created a school for bakers, and by the year 100BC there were said to be 258 bakeries in Rome. It is believed Emperor Cassius brought the first bread to Britain. Rotary millstones and watermills were built soon afterward to enable locals to produce their own flour and bread. But when the Romans left Britain, so did the baking knowledge... until the Normans arrived and revived the yeasted loaf. It was this knowledge that the Pilgrim Fathers took to North America.

Now, as you can see, we have been making bread in Britain for a long time and it hasn't always been cheap or, I should say, good value. In the nineteenth century, the tax on imported wheat was so high a single loaf cost a person's entire wages and the people revolted. The tax was abolished in 1846.

The twentieth century saw the start of the mass production of bread. More bread was made faster, but the process compromised both its quality and nutritional content. The domestic bread-making machine arrived at the end of the century, making it easier for home cooks to bake their own bread. Today, the emphasis is on whole grains, and wholegrain breads are the healthier choice.

LEFT PAGE CLOCKWISE FROM TOP LEFT:
pain de campagne rond, pain de campagne
long, baguette paysanne, pain paysan,
fougasse, fougasse aux céréales, pain de Meule

RIGHT PAGE CLOCKWISE FROM LEFT:
baguette artisanal, ficelle, ficelle aux céréales,
pain artisanal, pain de campagne aux noix,
pain de mie

The word "tapenade" comes from the Provençal word "tapeno," meaning capers, which are the traditional base for this tantalizing combination. You can make it in many different ways according to your taste, and some recipes from Provence use a larger proportion of capers to olives, but the one I like is made with black olives (from the South of France, if possible) and watercress leaves. It has a beautiful deep purple color and is full of flavor and complexity. It tastes great with crudités, on toasted bread with fresh tomatoes or even served alongside roast lamb or chicken.

Tapenade

TAPENADE

Preparation time 10 minutes

1½ cups small pitted black olives

1 canned anchovy fillet (optional)

½ cup olive oil

1 garlic clove

1 handful of watercress leaves, stems discarded

1 tablespoon capers, rinsed

Put all the ingredients in a food processor and process 3 to 4 minutes until the mixture forms a paste of the desired consistency.

Transfer to a small jar (the one the olives came in is ideal), cover with a lid and keep in the refrigerator. The tapenade will keep up to 2 weeks and will be better than anything you can buy!

VARIATION: GREEN OLIVE TAPENADE
If you want to try a variation, replace the black olives with green ones and replace the watercress with 1 handful of basil leaves.

Anchoïade

ANCHOIADE

Preparation time 15 minutes

7 ounces salted anchovy fillets

2 garlic cloves

1 teaspoon white wine vinegar

⅔ cup olive oil

freshly ground black pepper

Rinse the anchovy fillets well under cold running water, then pat dry using a clean dish towel.

Put the anchovy fillets, garlic and vinegar in a mortar or small food processor and season with pepper. Work everything together with the pestle or by processing until the mixture forms a paste. Slowly add the oil while continuing to mix. You should end up with a smooth, silky texture.

Transfer the anchoiade to a small jar, cover with a lid and keep in the refrigerator. It will keep up to 2 weeks.

Tomates séchées au four

OVEN-DRIED TOMATOES

Preparation time 10 minutes
Cooking time 3 hours

6 tablespoons olive oil, plus extra as needed

6 garlic cloves, unpeeled and crushed with the flat edge of a knife or your hand

1 pound 2 ounces cherry tomatoes

2 teaspoons confectioners' sugar

a few thyme or rosemary sprigs

sea salt and freshly ground black pepper

Heat the oven to 225°F. Put the oil and garlic in a small baking dish and leave to infuse in the oven 30 minutes, then remove the garlic. This gives you a lovely scented oil in which to roast your tomatoes. (Don't waste the garlic: once you've got the tomatoes in the oven, toast some crusty bread, drizzle it with olive oil and eat it with the garlic, which you can push out from its skin—it's incredible!)

Cut the tomatoes in half, across the middle rather than from top to bottom (they somehow look more appealing cut this way). Squeeze gently to remove some of the seeds and juice so they dry more easily, then put them skin-side down in the baking dish. Put the confectioners' sugar in a fine strainer and sprinkle it over the tomatoes, then season with salt and pepper. Toss the thyme sprigs over them and leave in the oven to dry 2 1/2 hours. Serve warm, or leave the tomatoes to cool, then remove the thyme sprigs, put the tomatoes in a jar and cover them with extra olive oil. They will keep in the refrigerator 2 to 3 weeks.

Caviar d'aubergine

EGGPLANT CAVIAR

Preparation time 15 minutes
Cooking time 1 hour

3 eggplants, halved lengthwise

6 tablespoons olive oil, plus extra as needed

6 garlic cloves, unpeeled and crushed with the flat edge of a knife or your hand

6 thyme or rosemary sprigs

sea salt and freshly ground black pepper

Heat the oven to 350°F. Using a sharp knife, score the flesh of the eggplants, making a crisscross pattern. Put them on a baking sheet, flesh-side up, drizzle with the oil and season with salt and pepper. Put 1 garlic clove and 1 thyme sprig on each eggplant half, cover with foil and bake 1 hour, or until the eggplants are very soft and the flesh is easy to scoop out.

Remove from the oven and discard the thyme. Peel the garlic cloves and put them on a cutting board. Scoop the flesh from the eggplants onto the board and discard the skins. Chop finely, mixing in the garlic, then season with salt and pepper and add a drop of oil, if liked.

Transfer the caviar to a jar, cover the surface with extra oil and cover with a lid. This will keep up to 1 week in the refrigerator.

You find yourself in Paris for a weekend, the sun is shining and you manage to get a seat on a terrace outside a brasserie on one of the wide boulevards. You are thinking you would like to watch the world go by for an hour or two and soak up the atmosphere. Maybe you'll have a snack … but what? No trip to Paris is complete without a Croque Monsieur. This is a twist on the traditional, call it Croque Monsieur Galmiche if you will. It is the way we used to do it at home for our Sunday night treat.

Croque Monsieur au jambon et comté

CROQUE MONSIEUR WITH HAM & COMTÉ CHEESE

Preparation time 15 minutes, plus making the salad and vinaigrette
Cooking time 5 minutes

4 extra-large eggs

1¾ cups whole milk

1 long *pain paysan* (or a farmhouse bread), cut diagonally into 8 thick slices

⅔ cup butter

8 slices of cooked ham

1 cup grated aged Comté cheese or other mature hard cheese

sea salt and freshly ground black pepper

corn salad tossed with French Vinaigrette (see page 20), to serve

Put the eggs and milk in a bowl, season with salt and pepper and whisk well, then transfer to a shallow dish. Soak each slice of bread in the egg mixture, turning three or four times so it really absorbs the liquid.

Melt half the butter in a large skillet over medium heat. When foaming, add the bread and cook 2 minutes, or until golden brown and a little crisp, then turn the bread over and add the rest of the butter. Cook on the other side for 2 minutes. If you are using a small skillet, cook in batches using one-quarter of the butter for each batch.

Put 1 slice of ham and some of the grated cheese on each slice of bread, and when the cheese starts to melt add another slice of bread on top of the cheese and flick the croque monsieur over once more and cook up to 1 minute, or until heated through. Serve hot with the salad. Perfect!

A creamier, richer alternative for Madame, with the simple addition of a fried egg and a couple spoonfuls of Béchamel sauce. Béchamel sauce owes its name to the Marquis of Béchamel, who felt it was an improvement on velouté (which is made in a similar way but, with white stock rather than milk), although it was originally made by simply adding large quantities of cream.

Croque Madame

CROQUE MADAME

Preparation time 5 minutes, plus making the Croque Monsieur and 20 minutes chilling
Cooking time 15 minutes

3 tablespoons butter, softened

⅓ cup all-purpose flour

1¾ cups milk

a pinch of freshly grated nutmeg

1 tablespoon sunflower oil

4 eggs

1 recipe quantity Croque Monsieur with Ham & Comté Cheese (see left)

sea salt and freshly ground black pepper

In a small bowl, mix the butter and flour together until the mixture forms a smooth paste, cover with plastic wrap and chill 20 minutes.

Put the milk and nutmeg in a saucepan and season with salt and pepper. Bring to a boil, then remove the pan from the heat and set aside to infuse and cool about 15 minutes.

Slowly reheat the milk over medium-low heat and add the butter and flour paste, little by little, until the milk thickens to a sauce. Stir continuously to make sure you get a lovely smooth texture without any lumps. This is known as a béchamel sauce.

Heat the broiler to medium-high. Meanwhile, make your Croque Monsieur according to the recipe directions.

To fry the eggs, heat a large skillet over medium heat, then add the sunflower oil. When it starts to smoke, break the eggs into the pan, without bursting the yolks, and fry until the whites are cooked and the edges crisp and golden.

Put 1 egg on top of each Croque Monsieur and pour a few spoonfuls of the béchamel sauce over each one. Broil 3 to 4 minutes until light golden brown.

Leeks make a great alternative to asparagus when it is out of season. These tasty vegetables belong to the same family as onions and garlic, but have a milder flavor, which works really well in this dish with vinaigrette. If you're using bigger, older leeks, cut the coarse, green part away and use only the white part. But if you've opted for younger, baby leeks, you can use the whole vegetable.

Poireaux à la vinaigrette

LEEKS WITH VINAIGRETTE

Preparation time 10 minutes, plus making the vinaigrette
Cooking time 20 minutes

1 teaspoon vinegar

2 eggs, at room temperature

4 leeks or 12 baby leeks

1 small handful of flat-leaf parsley, chopped

1 recipe quantity French Vinaigrette (see page 20)

sea salt

Fill a small saucepan with water and bring to a boil. Add the vinegar to the water, as this will make the eggs easier to shell after cooking. Place the eggs in a ladle, then slowly and carefully slide the eggs into the water so you don't break the shells. Simmer 8 to 9 minutes, drain and place the eggs under running cold water. When cool enough to handle, shell the eggs, roughly chop and set aside.

Bring another medium saucepan of salted water to a boil. Add the leeks and cook over medium heat 15 minutes. Drain and immediately plunge the leeks directly into cold water for a few seconds to stop the cooking process and keep the bright color. Don't leave them in the water for too long, because you want them still to be warm. Pat the leeks dry on a clean dish towel, then arrange on a flat serving dish.

Mix the chopped eggs and parsley into the vinaigrette, pour the mixture over the leeks and serve. Colorful, simple and delicious.

CHEF'S TIP: *When hard- or soft-boiling eggs, it is best to use the eggs at room temperature and not directly from the refrigerator, when the shells are more likely to crack as you add them to the boiling water.*

Late spring is the season of asparagus, both green and white; the best is whatever you can buy locally. Asparagus has quite a short season of seven or eight weeks, so make the most of this luxurious vegetable when it's available. I like to keep the flavors simple, such as in this dish, so you can really appreciate its freshness! The question with asparagus is always where to cut it; the way you can tell is by holding it from both ends and bending it—the spear will naturally snap between your fingers at just the right place.

Asperges à la vinaigrette au persil

ASPARAGUS WITH PARSLEY VINAIGRETTE

Preparation time 15 minutes
Cooking time 20 minutes

1 pound 2 ounces asparagus spears, woody ends discarded, peeled if tough

1 tablespoon sea salt

PARSLEY VINAIGRETTE

2 tablespoons white wine vinegar, plus extra to hard-boil the egg

1 egg, at room temperature

2 teaspoons Dijon mustard

7 tablespoons sunflower or olive oil

1 small handful of parsley, chopped

sea salt and freshly ground black pepper

Fill a small saucepan with water and bring to a boil. Add a teaspoon of vinegar to the water, because this will make the egg easier to shell after cooking. Place the egg in a ladle, then slowly and carefully slide the egg into the water so you don't break the shell. Cook 8 to 9 minutes, then drain and place the egg under running cold water. When cool enough to handle, shell the egg, chop roughly and set aside.

Bring another medium saucepan of water to a boil and add the salt. Tie up the asparagus loosely with string, tips all facing the same direction, and put the bundle in the pan, tips pointing upward. Reduce the heat to low and cook 6 to 10 minutes, depending on the size of the asparagus. The spears should be cooked through but still retain some bite.

Meanwhile, prepare a bowl of ice-cold water and set aside, then make the parsley vinaigrette. Put the mustard and vinegar in a bowl, season with salt and pepper and mix well. Slowly whisk or beat in the oil, then stir in the chopped egg and parsley.

When the asparagus is cooked, remove the bundle from the pan and plunge it into the ice-cold water. This helps to keep the chlorophyll (and, therefore, the goodness and color) locked in.

Untie the asparagus and drain it well, then arrange it on a flat dish. Pour the vinaigrette over and serve. This is a great dish to share with a friend, using nothing but your fingers—at least that is how we do it in France!

Asparagus, poached egg and hollandaise sauce—the perfect *ménage à trois*! Of course, you can often get hold of asparagus throughout the year, but it is always better when in season. Green works better than white for this dish, and rich, glossy, homemade hollandaise makes more difference than I can say.

Oeuf poché aux asperges et sauce hollandaise

POACHED EGG WITH ASPARAGUS & HOLLANDAISE SAUCE

Preparation time 10 minutes, plus making the sauce
Cooking time 15 minutes

2¼ pounds small to medium green asparagus spears, woody ends discarded, peeled if tough

4 tablespoons white wine vinegar

4 extra-large eggs

sea salt and freshly ground black pepper

1 recipe quantity Hollandaise Sauce (see page 20)

Bring a saucepan of salted water to a boil. Tie up the asparagus loosely with string, tips all facing the same direction, and put the bundle in the pan, with the tips pointing upward. Reduce the heat to low and cook 6 to 10 minutes, depending on the size of your asparagus. The spears should be cooked through but still retain some bite.

Meanwhile, prepare a bowl of ice-cold water and set aside. Bring another small saucepan of water to a boil, add the vinegar and bring it down to a simmer. Break 2 of the eggs into the pan (or just do one at a time if you still don't feel confident about poaching eggs). Swirl the water a little and keep simmering 4 minutes, or until the white surrounds the yolk in a nice oval shape. (You can manipulate it, using a spoon.) Alternatively, if you have an egg poacher, just use that.

When the asparagus is cooked, remove the bundle from the pan and plunge it into the ice-cold water. This helps to keep the chlorophyll (and, therefore, the goodness and color) locked in.

Untie the asparagus and drain it well, then divide it onto four plates. Top each portion with a poached egg, then with a dollop of the hollandaise sauce, so it just runs down the side of the egg onto the asparagus. Season with salt and pepper and serve immediately. I promise you, this is wonderful!

Crabe tiède avec mayonnaise à l'estragon

WARM CRAB WITH TARRAGON MAYONNAISE

*Preparation time 10 minutes, plus
making the vinaigrette
Cooking time 3 minutes*

3½ ounces cooked crabmeat

4 tablespoons mayonnaise

1 small handful of tarragon,
chopped

3 or 4 drops of chili sauce

sea salt and freshly ground black
pepper

seasonal mixed leaves, to serve

1 avocado, peeled, pitted and sliced,
to serve

1 recipe quantity French Vinaigrette
(see page 20), made with
wholegrain mustard

Put the crabmeat in a heatproof bowl and rest it over a saucepan of gently simmering water, making sure the bottom of the bowl does not touch the water. Heat over low heat 2 to 3 minutes, to warm the crab meat through, then remove the bowl from the heat and mix in the mayonnaise, tarragon and chili sauce and season with salt and pepper.

Serve warm with mixed leaves and sliced avocado, drizzled with the French vinaigrette.

Filet de maquereau au citron vert

MACKEREL WITH LIME (PICTURED)

*Preparation time 30 minutes, plus
1 hour marinating
Cooking time 7 minutes*

2 whole mackerel, about 14 ounces
each, filleted

4 tablespoons olive oil

1 kaffir lime leaf, cut into fine strips

a pinch of sea salt

a pinch of freshly ground black
pepper

1 lime, halved

Score the mackerel fillets slightly so the marinade really penetrates the flesh, then put them in a small dish. Add all the remaining ingredients except for the lime, cover with plastic wrap and leave to marinate 1 hour in the refrigerator.

Meanwhile, heat the oven to 350°F. Heat a small skillet over medium-high heat. Put the fish, skin-side down, on the pan and fry 2 minutes to give the fillets a nice color, then transfer them to a baking dish and roast 5 minutes.

Squeeze the lime over the mackerel and serve.

You can find this popular traditional dish on tables in almost every region of France, and in quite a few supermarkets, too—but it is never quite the same as homemade. There are so many recipes for what is often known simply as "pâté," but you need the right balance of liver and fat to make it both smooth and tasty, and some recipes have a very high percentage of fat, which isn't necessary or good for you. This terrine is complemented simply and beautifully by gherkins, pickled vegetables and farmhouse bread, making it a great dish for outdoor gatherings.

Terrine de foie de volaille

CHICKEN LIVER TERRINE

Preparation time 30 minutes, plus overnight soaking, 3 hours cooling and 2 days resting
Cooking time 1 hour 5 minutes

1 pound 2 ounces chicken livers, trimmed and all green parts removed

4¼ cups milk

1 tablespoon sea salt

4 tablespoons crème fraîche

1 garlic clove, crushed

a pinch of freshly grated nutmeg

2 tablespoons Cognac

4 eggs

4 egg yolks

⅔ cup cornstarch

⅔ cup butter

ground white pepper

gherkins, to serve

pickled vegetables, to serve

warm toasted bread, to serve

Put the livers in a large bowl and cover with 1 cup of the milk and 1 cup water. Sprinkle with the salt and leave to marinate in the refrigerator overnight, or at least 2 hours. Drain the livers, rinse under running water and put them on a clean dish towel to remove any excess liquid. Put the crème fraîche, garlic, nutmeg and remaining milk in a medium saucepan. Season with salt and white pepper and warm over low heat 5 minutes.

Heat the oven to 250°F. Put the livers and Cognac in a blender and blend 20 to 30 seconds. Add the eggs, egg yolks and cornstarch and blend 5 minutes longer, or until smooth and silky. While the blender is running, slowly add the milk mixture, a little at a time, covering the blender with the lid between additions and continuing to blend until all the liquid is incorporated.

Strain the mixture through a strainer into a 9¹/₂- x 4- x 3¹/₄-inch terrine mold (preferably cast iron). Cover with a piece of waxed paper cut to the size of the terrine, then put the mold's lid on top. Put the terrine in a deep baking dish and fill the dish with enough hot water to come two-thirds of the way up the sides of the terrine. Bake 1 hour, or until a knife inserted into the terrine comes out dry and hot when tested on sensitive skin, such as the inside of your wrist. Alternatively, until a thermometer inserted into the middle reads 154°F. Remove the terrine from the water and leave to cool at least 2 or 3 hours. It must be completely cool.

Melt the butter and pour it over the top of the cool terrine to prevent oxidation. Cover with plastic wrap and leave 2 days in the refrigerator to let the terrine set and the flavors concentrate. To serve, dip a knife in hot water and run it along the sides of the terrine mold, then put the mold in water 1 minute to help loosen it farther before unmolding onto a plate. Slice and serve with gherkins, pickled vegetables and warm, toasted bread.

Contrary to what people think, making a terrine isn't difficult, but it does take time—you usually need to make it at least two days in advance to make sure the flavors really develop and it sets properly. This recipe can be easily adapted to use game during the hunting season, if you like. It is also delicious made with young wild boar, pheasant, partridge, wild duck or deer.

Terrine de porc

PORK TERRINE

Preparation time 35 minutes, plus overnight marinating and 2 days resting
Cooking time 1 hour 30 minutes

10 ounces pork shoulder, cut into 1-inch cubes

10 ounces pork liver, ground

10 ounces pork neck, half cut into 1-inch cubes and half ground

10 ounces pork fat from belly, minced

3 tablespoons Armagnac

½ teaspoon freshly grated nutmeg

7 tablespoons dry white wine

¾ teaspoon salt

½ teaspoon ground white pepper

12 slices of smoked bacon

2 eggs

7 tablespoons heavy cream

¼ cup shelled unsalted pistachio nuts

2 thyme sprigs

pickled vegetables, to serve

bread, to serve

Twenty-four hours before cooking, chop the pork shoulder, pork liver, pork neck and pork fat until you have a coarse ground texture, then transfer to a large mixing bowl. Or pulse the meat in a food processor. If using a food processor, process one ingredient at a time before transferring it to the bowl. Mix in the Armagnac, nutmeg, wine, salt and white pepper, then cover with plastic wrap and marinate in the refrigerator overnight, or at least 3 hours.

Heat the oven to 250°F and remove the mixing bowl from the refrigerator. Cover the bottom and sides of a 9½- x 4- x 3¼-inch terrine mold (preferably cast iron) with the bacon, letting it hang over the sides, then set aside.

Now it is time to finish the terrine mixture. Whisk the eggs and cream together and gradually mix them into the meat, using a spatula. Once thoroughly mixed, add the pistachios. Transfer to the mold and pack the mixture down by pressing with the spatula or the back of a spoon. Put the thyme sprigs on top and cover with the overlapping bacon. Put the terrine in a deep baking dish and fill the dish with enough hot water to come two-thirds of the way up the sides of the terrine mold. Bake 1½ hours, or until a thermometer inserted into the middle reads 154°F. Alternatively, insert a knife into the terrine. It should come out dry and hot if tested on sensitive skin, such as the inside of your wrist or your lip.

Remove the terrine from the water and leave it to cool completely at room temperature with a 2¼- to 4-pound weight, such as a bag of sugar, on top. Place a piece of waxed paper between the terrine and the weight. Once cool, cover and leave in the refrigerator 2 days before serving to let the flavors develop. This resting time really enhances the flavor. Serve with pickled vegetables and bread.

Rillettes are prepared from cooked, shredded meat and are served in ways similar to pâté. Prepared rillettes are widely available from delicatessens in France, but they are also easy to make yourself—with the bonus that you get to use the meat or poultry of your choice. As well as the traditional pork belly, you can make rillettes from duck, goose, rabbit or even wild boar. Served with toasted baguette and with other charcuterie, they make an ideal appetizer.

Rillettes de canard

DUCK RILLETTES

Preparation time 30 minutes, plus overnight marinating and 1 day resting
Cooking time 6 hours

8 duck legs, about 5 ounces each

¼ cup sea salt

3 bay leaves

5 thyme sprigs, lightly crushed

3¼ pounds goose fat

a few whole black peppercorns (optional)

freshly ground black pepper

crusty bread, to serve

Put the duck legs in a bowl, skin-side down. Add the salt, 2 of the bay leaves and 4 of the thyme sprigs and season with pepper. Toss well, then cover with plastic wrap and marinate in the refrigerator overnight, or at least 2 hours. The longer you leave the duck to marinate, the more flavor your dish will have.

Heat the oven to 250°F. Briefly rinse the duck legs under cold running water to remove the excess salt, then drain on paper towels.

Melt the goose fat in a large cast-iron Dutch oven over low heat. Add the duck and toss until well coated, then transfer to the heated oven, uncovered, and cook, without stirring, 6 hours, or until the meat is falling easily from the bone. Remove the duck legs from the pan, discard the skin and bones and shred the meat into a mixing bowl, using a fork. Mix in a little of the warm goose fat to moisten.

Transfer the mixture to a sealable jar, or to a small earthenware dish, and press it down. Pour a film of goose fat over the top to seal it, then top with the remaining thyme sprig and bay leaf and a few whole peppercorns. Cover with waxed paper and refrigerate at least 24 hours before using to enhance the flavor. The remaining goose fat can be put in a jar and kept for other uses. Serve the rillettes with crusty bread.

As an alternative to my classic Goat Cheese Salad below, you can also try an even simpler version—it's also full of wonderful flavors! Simply stop at the supermarket and pick up a selection of green salad leaves, a loaf of bread and some goat cheese. Go home and make croutons with golden, melted goat cheese and a little walnut oil drizzled over the top. Serve with the fresh green salad and a glass of chilled white wine. *Santé!*

Salade de fromage de chèvre

GOAT CHEESE SALAD

Preparation time: 20 minutes, plus making the vinaigrette

1 yellow Belgian endive

1 head of radicchio

3 ounces arugula leaves

6 ounces goat cheese, such as Sainte-Maure de Touraine, Coeur de Lion La Buche or any other good-quality goat cheese

¼ cup chopped walnuts or hazelnuts

1 recipe quantity French Vinaigrette (see page 20)

Cut off the base and outer leaves of the Belgian endive, then cut in half, lengthwise, and remove the core. Cutt off the base and outer leaves of the radicchio, quarter lengthwise and remove the core. Arrange the endive and radicchio on four plates, with the arugula in the middle. Crumble the goat cheese over the salad and sprinkle with the walnuts. Drizzle with the dressing and serve.

CHEF'S TIP: *Add some hazelnut oil to your French Viniagrette, which makes the dressing less classic, but adds extra flavor to the salad. Also, to add extra depth of flavor to your salad, toast the nuts in a skillet over medium heat, tossing them often and watching them closely so they don't burn.*

Soufflé au fromage

CHEESE SOUFFLÉ

*Preparation time 40 minutes, plus
chilling and infusing
Cooking time 45 minutes*

4 tablespoons butter, softened

6½ tablespoons all-purpose flour

1¼ cups milk

1 bouquet garni, made with
   1 parsley sprig, 1 thyme sprig and
   1 small bay leaf, tied together with
   kitchen string

a pinch of freshly grated nutmeg

4 eggs, separated

¾ cup grated cheddar cheese

¾ cup grated Comté, or other hard
   cheese, plus extra for sprinkling

cayenne pepper (or paprika for a
   milder flavor), for sprinkling

a few drops of lemon juice

2 ounces mild, crumbly goat cheese,
   diced

sea salt and freshly ground black
   pepper

Mix 3 tablespoons and 1 teaspoon of the butter with the flour until the mixture forms a smooth paste. Transfer to a small dish, cover with plastic wrap and chill 20 minutes.

Meanwhile, put the milk, bouquet garni and nutmeg in a small saucepan and bring to a boil over high heat. Remove the pan from the heat and set aside to infuse and cool about 15 minutes, or until just warm.

Strain the milk mixture into a large saucepan and season with salt and pepper. Reheat gently over medium-low heat to a simmer, then add the butter and flour paste bit by bit, stirring until the milk thickens. It should have a very smooth texture without any lumps. Continue to cook the milk mixture 5 minutes longer, then add the egg yolks, one by one, stirring until combined after each addition. Add ²/₃ cup each of the cheddar and Comté cheeses and stir well. Season again with salt and pepper and set aside.

Grease four individual 3¹/₂- x 2-inch ramekins (or one round 7- x 3¹/₄-inch deep soufflé dish) with the remaining butter, then coat the inside of the dishes with the remaining cheddar and Comté cheeses, sprinkle a little cayenne pepper over and chill to set while you finish preparing the soufflé mixture.

Heat the oven to 375°F and rub a large clean bowl with the lemon juice, then wipe dry. Put the egg whites in the bowl and beat with a whisk or electric mixer until medium to stiff peaks form. Avoid overbeating or the mixture will split and the soufflés will collapse. Beat half the egg whites into the cheese mixture, then carefully fold in the rest, using a spatula, until smooth and firm but light.

Spoon half the mixture into the ramekin dishes, add the goat cheese and then top with the remaining soufflé mixture. Smooth the tops and wipe the inside borders of the dishes clean with your thumb. Finally, sprinkle a little extra Comté over.

Bake the soufflés in the heated oven 10 minutes (12 minutes if you are making one large soufflé), then lower the temperature to 325°F and bake 15 to 20 minutes longer until well risen, golden brown and slightly trembling. Switch the oven off and leave the soufflés in the oven 2 to 3 minutes longer, then remove from the oven and serve immediately.

Boeuf bourguignon

Foie de veau poêlé aux câpres, persil et cerfeuil

Steak au beurre d'herbes et citron

Boudin noir aux poires

Gigot d'agneau rôti à l'ail et lavande

Steak tartare

Cassoulet toulousain

Poulet au vin rouge

Les Viandes
MEAT, POULTRY & GAME

There is such a diverse selection of meat, poultry and game from all around France that the possibilities are endless. In most brasseries you will find the traditional favorites, popular all over the country, as well as specialties from the individual region, such as Roast Leg of Lamb with Garlic & Lavender in the south and classic Beef Bourguignon in Burgundy. Some of my personal favorites are from my home region. For me, you can't beat a farm-sourced Pork Steak with Mustard & Gherkin Sauce or Maman's Pot-Roasted Pheasant. This is real food—the food we love to eat. Eat to live or live to eat—no contest really!

There is so much you can do with the forgotten cuts of meat. Rump, oxtail, cheek and flap meat are good for a variety of uses, from minute steaks to stews, and they make a refreshing change from the classic tenderloin, sirloin or entrecôte. When growing up, we used to eat minute steaks and stews quite often. Maman always made them on Tuesdays, because that was market day and the meat was guaranteed to be fresh and of the highest quality. The classic minute steak is a terrific no-nonsense meal—it's great served with homemade fries and a seasonal salad or simply in a baguette with mustard.

Steak au beurre d'herbes et citron

STEAK WITH HERB & LEMON BUTTER

Preparation time 20 minutes, plus making the fries and salad
Cooking time 5 minutes

2 tablespoons sunflower oil

4 minute steaks, about 6 ounces each, flattened

1 tablespoon butter

sea salt and freshly ground black pepper

1 recipe quantity Large French Fries with Sea Salt (see page 165), to serve

seasonal salad, to serve

HERB & LEMON BUTTER

1 cup plus 2 tablespoons butter, softened

2 flat-leaf parsley sprigs, chopped

1 tarragon sprig, finely chopped

zest of 1 lemon

juice of ½ lemon

First, make the herb and lemon butter. Put the butter, herbs and lemon zest and juice in a bowl and season with salt and pepper. Mix together with a wooden spoon, then set aside 4 heaping teaspoons to use with the steaks.

Put a piece of plastic wrap on the countertop and spoon half the remaining lemon and herb butter along the middle. Wrap the plastic wrap around the butter and roll into a log shape. Repeat with the remaining butter, then wrap each log in a piece of foil and freeze. You can then cut pieces off at your convenience for use on barbecued, broiled or pan-fried meats.

Now make the steaks. Warm the oil in a large grill pan or skillet over medium heat. Season the steaks with salt and pepper and cook 2 minutes. Just before turning them, add the plain butter. Turn and cook the steaks 2 minutes longer. Do not let the butter burn, because it will give the meat a burned taste. It should be a lovely, light hazelnut color.

Put your steaks, piping hot, on a plate and top each one with 1 teaspoon of the reserved lemon and herb butter. Let it melt into the steaks a little, then serve with large french fries and a salad.

CHEF'S TIP: *To stop the edges of the steak from curling upward when being cooked, use a small, sharp knife to "nip" into the fat.*

This is an iconic French dish, and if you want to make it as the French do, you will probably use Charolais beef and a full-bodied Burgundy red wine. You don't need to use prime cuts of beef—the braising cuts, such as brisket, blade, cheek or even shank are most economical and give the dish much more flavor. In France, the process of cooking *boeuf bourguignon* often begins two days before serving, to soften the meat and conserve the aromas, but a three-hour marinade will do just as well.

Boeuf bourguignon

BEEF BOURGUIGNON

Preparation time 20 minutes, plus
3 hours marinating
Cooking time 2 hours 15 minutes

1¾ pounds beef brisket, cut into large cubes

4¼ cups full-bodied red wine

2 thyme sprigs

4 garlic cloves, crushed with the flat edge of a knife or your hand

3 tablespoons Cognac

scant ½ cup sunflower oil

2 tablespoons all-purpose flour

2½ cups veal stock or Chicken Stock (see page 18)

1 bouquet garni made with 1 parsley sprig, 1 thyme sprig and 1 small bay leaf, tied together with kitchen string

2 carrots, peeled, halved lengthwise and cut into chunks

12 silverskin or pearl onions

3 ounces small button mushrooms

⅔ cup diced pancetta

1 handful of flat-leaf parsley, roughly chopped

salt and freshly ground black pepper

1 recipe quantity Creamed Mashed Potatoes (see page 165), to serve

In a deep dish, mix together the beef, wine, thyme, garlic and Cognac. Cover with plastic wrap and leave to marinate in the refrigerator at least 3 hours.

Strain the meat into a bowl, using a colander, and reserve the marinade. Pat the meat dry.

Heat 4 tablespoons of the oil in a large saucepan or cast-iron Dutch oven over medium heat. Add the meat and cook 20 minutes, or until brown, season lightly with salt and pepper, then sprinkle with the flour and cook, stirring, 2 to 3 minutes longer. Add the stock and reserved marinade and bring to a boil. Skim the foam off the surface and add the bouquet garni, then reduce the heat to low and simmer, partially covered, 1 hour 45 minutes, stirring occasionally, or until the meat is tender. By that time you should have a rich, silky sauce.

About 50 minutes before the end of the cooking time, heat another medium saucepan with 1 tablespoon of the oil over medium-low heat. Add the carrots and onions and cook 10 minutes, or until soft and pale gold in color, then add to the pan with the meat.

When the beef is almost ready, heat the remaining oil in a skillet over medium heat. Add the mushrooms and pancetta and fry 8 to 10 minutes, stirring occasionally, until golden brown, then add them to the beef. Check the seasoning adjusting the salt and pepper, if necessary, throw in the parsley and stir gently without breaking the delicate pieces of beef.

Serve hot with creamed mashed potatoes for a perfect winter warmer.

The classic steak tartare is made without tomato sauce or egg yolk, but it was traditionally served with tartare sauce, which is where its name comes from. This famous dish first appeared in French restaurants in the early twentieth century and has remained popular ever since. As it is made from raw beef, it is very important to use top-quality meat. If you use beef tenderloin, choose the end part, and save the more expensive middle section for other uses. A cheaper cut I would recommend is sirloin, as it is as tender and tasty. Whichever cut you choose, however, make sure it is very fresh.

Steak tartare

STEAK TARTARE

Preparation time 20 minutes

1 small shallot, finely chopped

1 tablespoon chopped parsley leaves

1 tablespoon Dijon mustard

1 tablespoon tomato sauce

1 tablespoon capers, chopped

2 egg yolks

2 tablespoons olive oil

1 pound 5 ounces beef tenderloin or sirloin, trimmed of any sinew and cut into very small dice

sea salt and freshly ground black pepper

Mix the shallot, parsley, mustard, tomato sauce and capers in a medium-size bowl. Add the egg yolks, season with salt and pepper, then drizzle in the olive oil while still mixing. Finally, stir in the beef and check and adjust the seasoning.

Divide the mixture into 4 equal portions, shape into patties and serve.

CHEF'S TIP: *For variety, I also like to make this recipe using wasabi instead of mustard and a few drops of Worcestershire sauce.*

This dish is adored equally on both sides of the English Channel. It can be hard to find top-quality calf's liver, unless you know the farmer or your butcher has a good supplier, but it is well worth the search—calf's liver should be firm in texture and milky in color. The success of your dish depends both on the quality of the liver and the way in which you cook it. Here, it is simply pan-fried and served with a caper and herb butter, some delicious creamy mashed potatoes and warm, zesty buttered spinach. So easy to prepare, and really satisfying. I am a happy man.

Foie de veau poêlé aux câpres, persil et cerfeuil

PAN-FRIED CALF'S LIVER WITH CAPERS, PARSLEY & CHERVIL

Preparation time 15 minutes, plus making the potatoes and spinach
Cooking time 5 minutes

1¼ pounds calf's liver, cut into 4 equal pieces, each ½ inch thick

6 tablespoons butter

2 tablespoons chopped capers, rinsed

1 small handful of flat-leaf parsley, chopped

1 small handful of chervil, chopped

sea salt and freshly ground black pepper

1 recipe quantity Creamed Mashed Potatoes (see page 165), to serve

1 recipe quantity Buttered Spinach with Lemon Zest (see page 162), to serve

Put the calf's liver on some paper towels and pat dry to make sure it fries rather than boils.

Melt half the butter in a large skillet over medium heat. When it is a lovely golden color, add the liver to the pan and cook 2 minutes on each side, or until medium-rare to medium and golden brown on both sides. Remove the liver from the pan and keep warm.

Add the remaining butter to the pan, then add the capers, parsley and chervil, mixing with a wooden spoon. Season with salt and pepper, then pour the mixture over the liver. Serve hot with creamed mashed potatoes and buttered spinach.

It's funny the things that get us excited. For me it is the seasons—not just the colors and the smells, but knowing that soon certain produce is going to be available that hasn't been around for a while. When spring arrives, it is wild garlic first, then peas and, at last, the new season's spring lamb: milk-fed and unbelievably tender. Simply pan-roasted and served with zucchini, tomatoes and sauce vierge, this dish brings out all the freshness and color of the Mediterranean. Enjoy it with a light rosé wine, close your eyes and there you are—in Provence.

Agneau aux petits légumes et sauce vierge

ROAST LAMB WITH MEDITERRANEAN VEGETABLES & SAUCE VIERGE

Preparation time 20 minutes, plus making the sauce
Cooking time 30 minutes

2 lamb tenderloins, fully trimmed

4 rosemary sprigs

2 tablespoons olive oil

4 garlic cloves, unpeeled

salt and freshly ground black pepper

1 recipe quantity Sauce Vierge (see page 21), to serve

MEDITERRANEAN VEGETABLES

4 to 6 tablespoons olive oil

2 plum tomatoes, cut into ¼-inch-thick slices

2 small zucchini, cut into ¼-inch-thick slices

1 eggplant, cut into ¼-inch-thick slices

Heat the oven to 425°F. Season the lamb with salt and pepper, pierce each tenderloin on both sides with a sharp knife and insert a rosemary sprig into each opening. Heat a skillet with an ovenproof handle over medium heat and add the oil and garlic. Add the lamb and cook about 5 minutes, turning continuously, until sealed and golden brown all over. Transfer the skillet to the oven 5 to 8 minutes. Remove the skillet from the oven, set aside and keep the lamb warm.

Meanwhile, cook the vegetables. Heat another skillet over medium heat and add the oil. Add the vegetables in batches so they are in a single layer, season with salt and pepper and fry 3 to 4 minutes on each side until just tender and golden.

Starting with the tomatoes, arrange 3 slices of tomato and 2 slices of zucchini and eggplant, alternately and just overlapping, in the middle of each of four plates. Carve the lamb into thick slices on the diagonal and arrange on top of the vegetables. Spoon the sauce vierge over the lamb and around the plates and serve.

Why did I choose this dish? Simple—I love it! I think a lot of people feel the same way because it is delicious, easy to make and not too costly. The aromas that fill your kitchen are incredible, from the marinade right through to the roasting. Try to use herbs that are in season. In winter, use rosemary and thyme, for example, and in spring or summer, try *herbes de Provence*. If you are lucky enough to be able to pick fresh herbs, rub them in your hand before you throw them in the pot, because this helps release their essential oils. And don't forget to enjoy the fragrance left on your hand—it is a special moment when time stops for a few seconds, and you are glad to be exactly where you are.

Jarrets d'agneau braisés au vin rouge

LAMB SHANKS BRAISED IN RED WINE

Preparation time 20 minutes, plus making the stock, potatoes and ratatouille
Cooking time 2 hours 45 minutes

4 small lamb shanks

2 tablespoons sunflower oil

1 tablespoon olive oil

1 onion, cut lengthwise into 8 slices

2 carrots, peeled and chopped

1 celery stick, thinly sliced

2 tomatoes, quartered

1 garlic bulb, unpeeled and halved horizontally

3¼ cups full-bodied red wine

2 cups Lamb Stock (see page 18) or water

3 thyme or rosemary sprigs, or 1 small handful of mixed *herbes de Provence*

sea salt and freshly ground black pepper

1 recipe quantity Creamed Mashed Potatoes (see page 165), to serve

½ recipe quantity Ratatouille Provençale (see page 148), to serve

Put the lamb shanks on a plate and season well with salt and pepper, then rub the seasoning into the meat with your fingers. Heat the sunflower and olive oils in a cast-iron Dutch oven over medium to high heat. When the oils are hot but not burning, add the lamb shanks and cook, partially covered, 20 minutes, or until they turn a lovely golden brown color. Make sure the heat is high enough to seal the meat, but not burn it, and turn it frequently.

Add the onion, carrots, celery, tomatoes and garlic and cook, stirring frequently, 10 minutes longer, or until the vegetables are a light golden color. Add the wine, partially cover the pot and cook 5 minutes, or until the liquid reduces by half. This reduction helps to remove the acidity from the wine.

Add the stock and bring to a boil over high heat, then reduce the heat to low. Partially cover the pot with the lid, leaving a very small gap, and simmer 2 hours, or until the lamb is meltingly tender and the sauce reduces down a little. Keep an eye on the Dutch oven during cooking. Turn the meat from time to time and make sure it doesn't braise too fast and dry out—you want to have some sauce at the end.

About half an hour before your lamb is ready, add the herbs and partially cover again. I can already smell the mix simmering in the pot and gently wafting around the kitchen—what a joy!

Serve hot with creamed mashed potatoes and ratatouille.

CHEF'S TIP: *If by chance you find you have used a wine that is too acidic and you don't realize it until you taste the dish, add 1 teaspoon sugar. This will help rebalance the flavors.*

Rosemary and thyme are classic flavors to match with lamb, but lots of other herbs also go well with it. Personally, I find lavender wonderful. There are just two things to remember: measure it carefully (too much can make your food bitter) and only use the flowers, not the stems. A few years ago, while on vacation in Provence, we were walking into town to get some baguettes and *pains au chocolat* for breakfast when we found ourselves amid a sea of lavender fields. The color and aroma were truly magical. On the way back we picked huge bunches of it. Some we tied together to take home and dry, and some I decided to put in the pot … this is what I made.

Gigot d'agneau rôti à l'ail et lavande
ROAST LEG OF LAMB WITH GARLIC & LAVENDER

Preparation time 25 minutes, plus overnight marinating and making the potatoes
Cooking time 1 hour 10 minutes

3 pounds 5 ounces leg of lamb

1 garlic bulb, unpeeled and halved horizontally

8 lavender sprigs, flower heads only

⅔ cup olive oil

6 garlic cloves, peeled and halved

2 shallots, unpeeled and halved

sea salt and freshly ground black pepper

1 recipe quantity Sautéed Potatoes with Parsley & Garlic (see page 163), to serve

You need to begin this dish the day before you want to eat it. Put the lamb in a plastic-wrap-lined roasting pan that fits in the refrigerator and season with black pepper. (Don't season with salt now, because it draws the blood out of the lamb. Salt is always added just before cooking meat.) Add the garlic bulb and 6 heads of the lavender and pour 6 tablespoons of the oil over the top. Rub the seasonings in thoroughly, then wrap the lamb in the plastic wrap and leave in the refrigerator overnight.

Heat the oven to 400°F. Unwrap the lamb, put it back in the roasting pan with the garlic bulb and dab it with paper towels. Pierce it several times with a sharp knife and push a halved garlic clove inside each opening. Add the shallots to the pan, pour the remaining oil over the top, season with salt and pepper and then roast 1 hour, or until golden brown on the outside but still pink and moist inside. Remove the lamb from the pan, wrap it in foil to keep warm and set aside to rest.

Put 7 tablespoons water in the roasting pan to deglaze, then return it to the oven and cook 3 to 4 minutes until the water reduces. This gathers all the flavors from the caramelization of the meat and gives you the concentrated juice you need.

Unwrap the lamb. You will find some juice has also gathered in the foil—add it to the juice in the roasting pan, stir and set aside.

Slice the lamb, then drizzle it with the juice, sprinkle with the remaining lavender flowers and serve with sautéed potatoes with parsley and garlic.

CHEF'S TIP: *While lavender is an excellent match with the lamb, this dish can be made with more traditional herbs, such as rosemary and thyme, or any other herbs of your choice, to create your personal twist.*

Sauerkraut (*choucroute* in French) became popular when the first brasserie was opened in Paris by a brewer from Alsace, in northeastern France, in the late 1800s. Today, it is found on most, if not all brasserie menus right across France, and in some brasseries it will be served up more than a hundred times a day. It is one of those traditional recipes, rarely written down and yet somehow passed on from generation to generation, and there is probably no greater statement of Alsatian identity with regard to food than *choucroute alsacienne*. In this dish I team it with delicious smoked picnic ham and sausages to make a superbly flavorsome combination.

Choucroute alsacienne

SAUERKRAUT WITH PORK

Preparation time 40 minutes
Cooking time 3 hours

14 ounces picnic ham, smoked pork shoulder or pancetta

5 tablespoons duck fat

1 onion, chopped

2¼ pounds sauerkraut, drained, rinsed and gently pressed to remove any liquid

1 bouquet garni made with 1 small handful of parsley, 1 thyme sprig and 1 bay leaf, tied together with kitchen string

1 spice sachet with 4 juniper berries, 1 clove and a small pinch of cumin seeds, tied up in a small piece of cheesecloth

7 ounces pork belly

4¼ cups bottled lager

1 tablespoon vegetable bouillon powder

2 smoked German sausages, such as Strasbourg or Frankfurter

4 potatoes, peeled and cut in half

sea salt and freshly ground black pepper

mustard, to serve (optional)

Heat a heavy skillet over medium-high heat and cook the picnic ham, turning continuously, about 10 minutes until each piece has an even color all over. Remove the skillet from the heat and set aside.

Heat the duck fat in a large saucepan over medium heat. Add the onion and cook, covered, 5 minutes, stirring occasionally, until translucent but not colored. Add the sauerkraut, bouquet garni, spice sachet, sealed picnic ham and pork belly, lager and bouillon powder, then cover and cook over medium-low heat 1¹/2 hours. Check regularly and stir occasionally so the ingredients do not burn and stick to the bottom of the pan.

Uncover the pan, add the sausages, re-cover and cook 30 minutes longer. Add the potatoes and then cook 20 minutes longer, or until the potatoes are tender, making sure there is still a bit of liquid in the pan. If the liquid is too low, add 1 cup water.

Remove the pan from the heat and take out the bouquet garni and spice sachet. Season with salt and pepper, then transfer the sauerkraut to a large serving dish. Cut the meat, sausages and potatoes into serving pieces and serve on top of the sauerkraut. You can also have some mustard on the side, which is especially delicious with the sausages.

I love pork and the moisture and flavor of its delicate fat. If you buy it trimmed of fat, you buy it trimmed of flavor! The meat also dries out and loses its goodness. Animals raised as free-range have a far more varied diet, which makes their meat deliciously succulent—perhaps we notice the improvement in succulence with free-range pigs more because they are bred to be fatter than other animals. For me, the fattier cuts, such as pork belly, are best roasted first and then braised long and slow. I promise, they are well worth the wait.

Poitrine de porc confite aux pommes

PORK BELLY CONFIT WITH APPLES

Preparation time 25 minutes, plus overnight marinating and making the cabbage and potatoes
Cooking time 4 hours 30 minutes

juice of 1 lemon

2¼ pounds apples

2¾ pounds skinless, boneless pork belly, fat layer on

6 tablespoons sunflower oil

1 tablespoon butter

1 recipe quantity Braised Cabbage, (see page 158), to serve

1 recipe quantity Fondant Potatoes with Confit of Garlic (see page 164), to serve

MARINADE

3 carrots, peeled and halved lengthwise

3 onions, quartered

4 thyme sprigs

1 cinnamon stick, halved

1 star anise, halved

4 tablespoons sea salt

5 cups hard cider

freshly ground black pepper

First, put the lemon juice in a bowl of water and set aside. Peel the apples, reserving the skins for the marinade, then dip the fruit in the lemon water to prevent oxidation. Wrap the apples in paper towels, then place in a dish, cover with plastic wrap and set aside in the refrigerator.

In another bowl, mix together the reserved apple skins and all the marinade ingredients, except the cider. Put half of this mixture in a large roasting pan lined with kitchen foil. Put the pork belly on top, then cover with the remaining marinade mixture. Pour the cider over, cover with a sheet of waxed paper and leave to marinate in the refrigerator overnight.

Heat the oven to 275°F. Remove the pork from the marinade and dry it on a clean dish towel. Warm the sunflower oil in a large skillet over medium heat and cook the pork 18 to 20 minutes, turning occasionally, until golden brown but not crisp or burned.

Meanwhile, transfer the marinade to a saucepan, bring it to a boil over high heat and skim it with a slotted spoon to remove any foam that rises to the surface. Return the pork to the roasting pan and pour the marinade over. Cover with waxed paper to prevent the top from drying and cook 4 hours, or until the meat is very soft. You can check this by sliding a pointed knife through the meat.

When the pork is almost ready, cut each peeled apple into 4 or 6 wedges. Melt the butter in a skillet over medium heat and sauté the apples 6 to 8 minutes until golden brown.

Transfer the meat to a cutting board, cut into portions and serve warm with the apples, braised cabbage and fondant potatoes.

CHEF'S TIP: *If you have any leftover pork, cover it with waxed paper and keep refrigerated. Serve the following day as a cold meat appetizer with pickles, mustard and country-style bread.*

If you are concerned about the fat content of cuts such as pork belly, pork blade steak is a delicious, lower-fat alternative. One of the things I love about pork is how versatile it is. It can accommodate so many flavors, so many different spices and be cooked in so many ways: broiled, grilled, roasted, stir-fried or stewed. It can even be served cold with mustard on baguette. Its succulence and flavor make it perfect every time. It is always important to balance dishes well, which is why I like this one so much—the richness of the cream and pork are offset beautifully by the sharpness of the gherkin and mustard sauce.

Côtes de porc, sauce moutarde et cornichons

PORK STEAKS WITH MUSTARD & GHERKIN SAUCE

Preparation time 10 minutes, plus making the potatoes
Cooking time 15 minutes

2 tablespoons sunflower oil

4 pork blade steaks, about 5 ounces each

2 tablespoons butter

5 tablespoons light cream

1 teaspoon wholegrain mustard

1 tarragon sprig

4 small gherkins, halved and sliced into strips

sea salt and freshly ground black pepper

1 recipe quantity Creamed Mashed Potatoes (see page 165), to serve

Heat the oven to 275°F. Warm the oil in a nonstick skillet over medium heat. Add the steaks and fry 3 to 4 minutes on each side until golden brown, adding the butter when you turn them over. Remove the steaks from the pan and keep them warm in the oven.

Add 4 tablespoons water to the pan to deglaze. You should end up with a pale golden liquid. Bring to a simmer over low heat and slowly stir in the cream and mustard. Add the tarragon and gherkins and season with salt and pepper.

Divide the steaks onto four plates, pour the sauce over and serve immediately with creamed mashed potatoes—they are perfect for soaking up the sauce.

Originating from Castelnaudary in the fourteenth century, cassoulet is a gorgeous, satisfying, slowly simmered casserole. It is one of the best-known French dishes worldwide and is probably as near as you will get to a French National Dish. Haricot beans are at the heart of it, with the addition of meat or poultry of some kind, although never chicken or fish. In some cities it is made with pork, in others with mutton, goose or duck and, during the shooting season, game birds are also used. By the way, the name "cassoulet" comes from the word "*cassole*," a glazed earthenware pot especially designed to cook this dish in.

Cassoulet toulousain

TOULOUSE CASSOULET

Preparation time 25 minutes, plus soaking the beans
Cooking time 5 hours 15 minutes

1½ cups dried white haricot beans, such as cannellini, great northern or navy beans

1 clove

2 onions, 1 peeled and left whole and 1 chopped

3½ ounces pork rind

10 ounces pork belly or pork shoulder, skin removed

4 garlic cloves

4 tablespoons duck fat

14 ounces blade steak

2 carrots, peeled and chopped

1 bouquet garni made with 1 parsley sprig, 1 thyme sprig and 1 bay leaf, tied together with kitchen string

4 tablespoons tomato paste

4 Toulouse sausages

1½ cups fresh white bread crumbs

sea salt and freshly ground pepper

Put the beans in a bowl, cover with water and leave to soak for 20 minutes. Meanwhile, insert the clove into the whole onion and set aside.

Rinse the beans in cold water and drain, then transfer into a large Dutch oven. Add the clove-stuffed onion, pork rind, pork belly and garlic, then add enough water to cover all the ingredients completely. Partially cover the Dutch oven and place over medium heat. Bring to a very gentle simmer, reduce the heat to low and simmer up to 2½ hours, or until the meat is tender and the beans are cooked but still slightly firm. When the beans are ready, season with salt and pepper and remove the Dutch oven from the heat. Cut the pork belly into serving portions, then return them to the pot and set it aside, uncovered.

Meanwhile, after the bean mixture has been cooking for 2 hours, heat the duck fat in a large flameproof earthenware dish or large, deep saucepan over medium heat. Add the blade steak and fry 8 to 10 minutes until golden brown, then add the chopped onion, carrots and bouquet garni. Add about half of the liquid from the bean mixture, then top up with enough water to cover all the ingredients completely. Stir in the tomato paste. Cover and place over medium-low heat and simmer for 2 hours, or until the pork is very tender, then add the sausages and cook 30 minutes longer.

Heat the oven to 350°F. Remove the pork blade and sausages from the earthenware dish and put them in a large baking dish. Pour the bean mixture and liquid from the dish with the blade steak over them and sprinkle with the bread crumbs. Bake 30 minutes in the heated oven until the sauce thickens slightly and the top is golden brown.

The sausage-making tradition in France has lasted more than 2,000 years, and blood sausage, or *boudin noir*, is one of the oldest charcuterie preparations. It is very perishable, so it is produced on a daily basis in French *charcuteries*, and it should be used on the day you buy it for that reason. Each *charcuterie* will make it in a slightly different way from the other: different seasonings, fruit and vegetables will be used and some might add chestnuts and various aromatic ingredients. Yet, however blood sausages are made, they are incredibly popular both in brasseries and at home. I sometimes like to serve it with apples or quince, but I particularly enjoy it with pear as I have done here.

Boudin noir aux poires

BLOOD SAUSAGE WITH PEARS

Preparation time 20 minutes
Cooking time 25 minutes

1 pound 5 ounces blood sausage

4 teaspoons butter

2 large pears, peeled, cored and cut into 16 wedges

1 shallot, finely sliced

1 tablespoon brown sugar

2 tablespoons reduced balsamic vinegar

1 tablespoon sunflower oil

Bring a saucepan of salted water to a boil over medium heat, then add the blood sausage and simmer 2 to 3 minutes. Remove the pan from the heat and set aside. It is not imperative you prepare the blood sausage this way, but it will help prevent it from splitting open.

Melt the butter in a medium skillet over medium heat. Add the pears and cook 3 to 4 minutes until a pale, golden brown. Add the shallot and cook about 4 minutes, or until softened, then add the sugar, balsamic vinegar and 3 tablespoons water. Cook 2 to 3 minutes until the mixture has the consistency of a runny syrup. The pear wedges should still retain their shape and not be too soft. Remove the skillet from the heat and set aside.

Cut the blood sausage into approximately 1/4-inch-thick slices. Heat the sunflower oil in another medium-size skillet over low heat. Add the blood sausage slices and fry 6 to 8 minutes until brown on both sides and warm throughout. You do not want to cook it too fast or it will burst.

To serve, divide the shallot mix from the pan with the pears onto four plates. Arrange the blood sausages on the plates and then the pears. Spoon any remaining syrup over.

La Charcuterie
Charcuterie

The word "charcuterie" originated from the French term *chair cuite*, or "cooked meat." Today, it has come to mean the art and science of the pig—in other words, the butchering, fabrication and preparation of pork—but it is also a term used more generally for all sorts of cold meat, poultry and fish products and prepared dishes.

At home, we often had charcuterie of cold meat with fresh baguette, gherkins and radishes. This was our usual appetizer in spring and summer, and we loved it. Then came the main course, which might have been a picnic ham, roasted and then braised with cabbage or turnip. In Lure, my hometown, every Tuesday was market day, when the large town square was filled with local producers selling livestock. You could choose your pig, hen, duck, turkey, rabbit and a lot more for your dinner or for your farm. Once a month, farmers from all over the county came to the market to meet, make deals and buy livestock. I used to walk among them and listen to the stories they told. Sometimes, big arguments would break out, and in the regional dialect, too, which was so hard to understand. There was never a dull moment.

My family always bought from the same *charcutier*. Maman and Papa liked his products, and as he came from near Maman's village, he was almost a friend. He always reserved stuff for us and gave us something extra to eat and try, whether it was salami, or a specialty, such as *cervelas* (a cooked sausage from Alsace, often served in salad or simply broiled), which was full of garlic but so good. Several years later, when I was starting my apprenticeship at a hotel in the town of Luxeuil-les-Bains, I learned how to make a few of the charcuterie products I used to eat. Maman's and Papa's *charcutier* supplied the hotel. The hotel and the *chef patron* had a tremendous reputation in the region and everything was homemade. During my training I often had to prep the fowls, rabbit, deer or other animals before I started to make a dish. It wasn't easy, but I was learning—after all, that was why I was there.

One of the most important charcuterie dishes I learned to make were terrines: a mixture of meat, fish, poultry or seafood, packed into rectangular dishes and often cooked in a bain-marie. Usually served in the container in which they were made and accompanied by pickles or even a sauce, they formed part of a buffet display. Another form of charcuterie I learned how to make was pâté, often *en croûte* (in pastry). This is a rich meat, game or fish mixture baked in a pastry crust (usually puff pastry), which can be served hot or cold as an appetizer, as part of a cold buffet or as a meal in itself. Today, there is an abundance of different pâtés to choose from, with ingredients including chestnuts, red wine, herbs and spices. Other important charcuterie dishes in my region are *rillettes*, a preparation of pork, rabbit, goose or duck meat chopped, salted, cooked in goose fat and then pounded to a paste and potted (great on toast!); and *boudin noir*, or blood sausage, a savory sausage consisting largely of pork blood and fat, seasoned and contained in intestine, which forms the casing. Butchers in France all have their own recipes for this, which vary from adding onion and seasoning to including fruit, vegetables, herbs, cream, semolina, bread crumbs and so on. In my region, they add milk and onions. *Boudin noir* is delicious fried with pears or apples and served with mashed potatoes.

I was lucky to have such rigorous training, and, thankfully, many artisan producers are going back to the basics, and people love it. In the Vosges area, there are now plenty of *fermes-auberges*, farmhouse inns, where the owners rear their own animals and grow their own produce to sell in their stores and to use in their kitchens.

Such stores are always full and they offer great value for money. Word of mouth brings people from all over to sample their products. Charcuterie features heavily, of course, and here you can find and enjoy all the regional specialties, from *Rosette de Lyon* salami (an exquisite, cured *saucisson* made with finely ground pork from animals that live on a pure vegetarian diet) to *Saucisse de Toulouse* (a traditional sausage from Toulouse made with coarsely diced pork and flavored with wine, garlic and seasonings), which tastes great in cassoulet. I should also give a special mention to foie gras terrine, which is very popular during the festive season in France. A rare delicacy for food lovers, but a sensitive subject in general, it is made with goose or duck livers.

No discussion of charcuterie would be complete without mentioning pancetta, the cured, spiced pork belly that adds so much flavor to many recipes, and the many delicious types of ham there are to enjoy. There is *jambon cuit* (classic cooked ham), which is baked very slowly overnight in a low oven and traditionally kept in its brine for a few weeks, as well as tender *jambon cru* (uncooked ham), such as *Jambon de Luxeuil*. Similar to Bayonne ham, this is pickled in brine, dried, sometimes smoked and matured for a month before being used.

Charcuterie products are the ideal foods for eating with family and friends. There is a huge range of regional specialties to explore and enjoy, many of which have found their way onto brasserie menus. I have included my favorites in this book and invite you to share them. *Bon appétit!*

A BRIEF HISTORY OF CHARCUTERIE

An ancient art that commenced nearly 6,000 years ago, charcuterie became popular during the Roman empire when food started to become sophisticated. Since then, it has spread to many countries with diverse traditions and myriad culinary methods.

Charcuterie was extremely popular in France during the Middle Ages, when the country acquired many varieties of meat loaves, sausages and other meat products that were prepared and sold in specialist stores called *charcuteries*, owned and run by *charcutiers*, who needed the talent to season and cook delicious food and present it well to attract customers. They experimented with different meats and game, resulting in new foods for their customers. This created a lot of competition. The popular products and processes spread from France to neighboring regions, including Germany. Frankfurt became famous for the "frankfurter," a smoked sausage that evolved into the hot dog, while Genoa, in Italy, became renowned for its salami.

Now, more than 500 years later, you still find such foods in local and regional supermarkets. Stop at a freeway restaurant or food store in France and you are likely to find charcuterie in all its forms, from packaged goods to freshly made products, ready to buy and consume on the spot. If you happen to cross France from north to south or east to west, you will be able to learn a lot about each region simply by paying attention to what is on offer to eat at that time of year. Like cheeses and regional recipes, the range of charcuterie is vast, but each region claims the authenticity of their dishes or specialties. My region, Franche-Comté, is bordered by Alsace, the Vosges, Jura, Burgundy and Germany, so there are dozens of specialties. One of the best known is *saucisse de Morteau*, from Morteau, in Doubs, a smoked sausage made from a mixture of ground, seasoned meats. Traditionally, it is smoked in Tuyé chimneys, found in houses typical of the region. This sausage is cooked in boiling water or braised before you eat it and is delicious with lentils. Other specialties include *jambon fumé* (smoked ham) from Luxeuil-les-Bains, and *palette fumée* (tripe sausage), from the Vosges region. Luckily, all of these regional foods have entered the world of the brasserie, so you can enjoy them almost anywhere in France.

LEFT PAGE CLOCKWISE FROM TOP LEFT:
jambon de Bayonne, bûchettes de saucisson,
saucisson de Bigorre, lomo, saucisse au
piment

RIGHT PAGE CLOCKWISE FROM TOP
LEFT: boudin noir (blood sausage), salami,
chorizo, terrine de porc, coppa des Pyrénées,
ventrèche (pancetta), magret de canard fumé
(smoked duck breast)

This dish is my variation on *coq au vin*, which is such a classic it can be found in almost every brasserie in every region of France. The difference between one *coq au vin* and another is very subtle: the wine used will most likely be one from that region, and some cooks use more heavily smoked bacon than others. But, it is generally agreed you can't improve on perfection, so no one tries. Classic *coq au vin* has mushrooms in it and small onions rather than shallots, so my dish is called a casserole, not a *coq au vin*.

Poulet au vin rouge

CHICKEN CASSEROLE IN RED WINE

Preparation time 20 minutes, plus making the stock and cooking the tagliatelle
Cooking time 1 hour 15 minutes

2 to 3 tablespoons all-purpose flour, for dusting

1 chicken, about 3 pounds 5 ounces, cut into 8 pieces

1 tablespoon sunflower oil

1 shallot, chopped

1 ounce pancetta

2 large carrots, peeled and sliced

2 garlic cloves, unpeeled and crushed with the flat edge of a knife or your hand

1½ cups Burgundy red wine, or your choice of regional red table wine

2½ cups Chicken Stock (see page 18)

4 tablespoons butter, diced

1 handful of tarragon, leaves only, or 3 or 4 thyme sprigs

sea salt and freshly ground black pepper

tagliatelle, cooked, to serve (optional)

Sprinkle the flour onto a plate, season with salt and pepper and toss the chicken through the flour until it is lightly coated, then set aside. (The flour will help the sauce thicken while it's cooking.) Heat the oil in a Dutch oven over medium heat. Add the shallot, pancetta, carrots and garlic and cook 5 minutes, or until soft but not colored, then remove the ingredients from the pan and set aside.

Add the chicken to the Dutch oven and cook in the fat remaining in the pan over medium heat 8 to 10 minutes, turning as necessary, until it has an even color all around. Add the wine and cook 10 to 12 minutes until it reduces by half. Add the stock and the shallot mixture and bring to a boil over high heat. Skim the surface to remove any fat, then reduce the heat to low and cook, partially covered, 15 to 20 minutes.

Remove the chicken from the Dutch oven and set aside. Simmer the cooking liquid, uncovered, over medium heat 12 to 15 minutes until it reduces and turns into a lovely, light shiny syrup. Remove the Dutch oven from the heat and stir in the butter until it melts and is combined. Return the chicken to the pot and add the tarragon, keeping aside a few sprigs to sprinkle on top when serving.

Serve immediately with fresh tagliatelle, if liked.

Blancs de poulet au ragoût de petits légumes et lardons

PAN-FRIED CHICKEN WITH GARDEN VEGETABLE & PANCETTA RAGOUT

*Preparation time 20 minutes, plus
making the stock
Cooking time 1 hour*

3 pounds 5 ounces fava beans
    in the pods and then shelled,
    or 2 cups shelled fava beans

2 tablespoons sunflower oil

4 chicken breast halves on the bone,
    about 6 ounces each

4 tablespoons butter

2 garlic cloves, unpeeled and
    crushed with the flat edge
    of a knife or your hand

1 small handful of summer savory
    (*sarriette*) or 2 thyme sprigs

14 scallions, white bulbs only and
    roots cut off

a pinch of sugar

⅔ cup diced pancetta

1 teaspoon thyme leaves

¼ cup Chicken Stock (see page 18)
    or water

sea salt and freshly ground black
    pepper

Bring a saucepan of lightly salted water to a boil. Add the fava beans and blanch 20 seconds, then drain and refresh immediately in a bowl of ice-cold water and drain again. Peel the beans and discard the outer skins. I know it's a fiddly job, but it's worth the trouble, because it changes the flavor completely. Set aside the beans for your ragout.

Warm the oil in a large heavy-bottomed skillet or cast-iron pan over medium heat. Season the chicken with salt and pepper and cook, skin-side down and partially covered, 8 minutes, or until golden brown and slightly crisp. Turn the chicken over and add a tablespoon of the butter along with the garlic and summer savory sprigs. Reduce the heat to low and cook 8 minutes longer. Transfer to a serving dish, cover with kitchen foil and keep warm. Set the pan aside for making the jus later.

To make the ragout, melt a tablespoon of butter in a small skillet over medium heat. Add the scallions and cook, stirring frequently, 5 to 6 minutes until light golden. Season with salt and pepper and sprinkle in the sugar. Add 4 tablespoons water and cook over low heat, partially covered, 12 to 15 minutes until the water almost evaporates and the scallions are lightly glazed.

Meanwhile, bring a saucepan of water to a boil. Add the pancetta and blanch 1 to 2 minutes, then drain, refresh immediately in a bowl of cold water and drain again. Don't be tempted to blanch the pancetta any longer or it will turn too dry. Pat it dry with paper towels.

Sauté the pancetta in a medium skillet over medium heat about 4 minutes until slightly crisp. Stir in the fava beans, scallions and thyme and keep warm.

To make the jus, add the stock to the pan you roasted the chicken in and simmer 2 minutes over medium-low heat, then add the juices that will have collected under your chicken and stir in the remaining butter to give it a velvety shine.

Remove the chicken breasts from the bone, cut each of them into thick slices and arrange on four plates. Divide the ragout onto the plates, spoon the jus over and serve.

Poule au pot, sauce gribiche

POACHED CHICKEN WITH SAUCE GRIBICHE

Preparation time 1 hour
Cooking time 1 hour 25 minutes

1 chicken, 3 pounds 5 ounces
    to 4 pounds

1 tarragon sprig

1 bouquet garni made with
    2 parsley sprigs, 1 thyme sprig and
    1 small bay leaf, tied together with
    kitchen string

1 celery stick, peeled and cut in half

4 large carrots, peeled and cut in
    half lengthwise

2 leeks, washed, cut in half
    lengthwise and tied together

2 small turnips, peeled and cut
    in half

1 small cabbage, cut into quarters

4 cloves

2 small onions, cut in half

sea salt and freshly ground black
    pepper

bread, to serve

SAUCE GRIBICHE

1 teaspoon white wine vinegar, plus
    1 teaspoon for hard-boiling the
    eggs

4 eggs

1 teaspoon Dijon mustard

1 cup sunflower oil or light olive oil

¼ cup chopped gherkins

¼ cup capers, rinsed and chopped

1 flat-leaf parsley sprig, leaves only,
    finely chopped

1 tarragon sprig, leaves only, finely
    chopped

1 chervil sprig, leaves only, finely
    chopped

Put the chicken in a large saucepan, season with a handful of sea salt and cover with water. Bring to a boil over high heat, then skim the foam that rises to the top, using a ladle. Reduce the heat so the chicken is only simmering, then add the tarragon, bouquet garni, celery, carrots, leeks, turnips and cabbage. Push a clove into each of the onion halves and add them to the saucepan. Cook the chicken 1¼ hours, or until the meat is very tender and falling off the bone.

Meanwhile, make the sauce gribiche. Fill a small saucepan with water and bring to a boil. Add 1 teaspoon of vinegar to the water, because this will make the eggs easier to shell after cooking. Place 1 egg in a ladle, then slowly and carefully slide the egg into the water so you don't break the shell. Repeat for the remaining 3 eggs. Cook 8 to 9 minutes until hard-boiled, then drain and place the eggs under running cold water. When cool enough to handle, shell the eggs and cut in half.

Using a mortar and pestle or a food processor, mash the hard-boiled egg yolks until they form a smooth paste. Mix in the mustard and season with salt and pepper. While still mixing, add the vinegar, then slowly add the oil until the consistency resembles mayonnaise. Fold the gherkins, capers and herbs into the mixture and adjust the salt and pepper, if necessary. Finely chop the cooked egg whites and add them to the sauce. If you like, this sauce can be made the night before and chilled in the refrigerator.

Now it is time to enjoy. Serve the broth as a first course with a chunky piece of bread—it is really good—then remove the chicken from the pan and cut it into pieces. Serve with the vegetables and Sauce Gribiche.

CHEF'S TIP: *You can replace the chicken with a piece of braising beef or even pork. For the best results, I recommend top side or brisket for the beef, and the belly or blade steak for the pork. And if you like marrow, even better. It's great for serving with the beef.*

This is another very French salad found on every brasserie menu. It is very refreshing, with a nice crunch. You can use chervil instead of the tarragon; it is a wonderful herb that should be grown and used more often! Another delicious alternative is to use Saffron Mayonnaise (see page 21) instead of the garlic-flavored mayonnaise and flat-leaf parsley instead of tarragon.

Salade de blancs de volaille grillés

CHARGRILLED CHICKEN SALAD

Preparation time 35 minutes, plus 20 minutes marinating
Cooking time 15 minutes

4 chicken breast halves, skin on

olive oil, for seasoning

1 teaspoon vinegar

8 quail eggs

2 tablespoons garlic-flavored mayonnaise

2 tablespoons chopped tarragon

juice of 1 small lemon

1 romaine lettuce, cut into large pieces

2 tablespoons croutons

sea salt and freshly ground black pepper

Put the chicken breast halves in a small dish, season with salt and pepper and drizzle with olive oil. Cover with plastic wrap and leave to marinate 15 to 20 minutes.

Meanwhile, soft-boil the quail eggs. Fill a small saucepan with water and bring to a boil. Add the vinegar to the water, because this will make the eggs easier to shell after cooking. Place the eggs in a ladle, then slowly and carefully slide them into the water so you don't break the shells. Cook 4 minutes, then drain and cool the eggs under running cold water. When cool enough to handle, shell the eggs, cut them in half and set aside.

Heat the oven to 400°F. Heat a ridged cast-iron skillet or grill pan over medium heat and grill the chicken breasts, skin-side down, 5 minutes, then turn them over and grill 5 minutes longer. Your chicken breasts should now have charred grill marks on both sides. Transfer to a baking dish and roast in the heated oven 10 minutes longer.

Meanwhile, put the mayonnaise, tarragon and lemon juice in a large serving bowl, season with salt and pepper and mix well. Add the lettuce and mix.

Remove the chicken from the oven and cut it into thick slices while it is still warm. Arrange the slices on top of the salad and top with the quail eggs and finally the croutons. Serve warm.

It was Grand-Mère Suzanne who taught me how to make food for the chickens on the farm—baked potatoes, still warm, crushed together with grain and water by hand. I can still remember how sore my hands would get after a while. Once made, we would put the mix in the tray and call the chickens by shouting "*piu, piu, piu.*" They would all charge over, clucking in anticipation. When the chickens had devoured the mix, we would throw them some corn, too. All this was done twice a day— now that's the way to treat chickens! We fed them well, knowing one day they were going to feed us. When it was time to put them in the pot we didn't feel too sad, because we knew it was just nature taking its course. This is a very traditional recipe, normally prepared with baby chicken called *poussin*, however, you can also use guinea fowl—an often forgotten poultry that is very delicious. Here I've used one larger chicken to serve four.

Poulet fermier à la crapaudine
SPATCHCOCKED CHICKEN

Preparation time 30 minutes
Cooking time 50 minutes

1 small chicken, about 2¾ pounds, cut in half along both sides of the backbone, but kept as a whole piece

2 tablespoons olive oil

7 tablespoons butter, melted

Dijon mustard or wasabi paste, for brushing (optional)

1 cup fresh bread crumbs

sea salt and freshly ground black pepper

chili-flavored olive oil, to serve

Heat the oven to 400°F. Place the chicken on a cutting board, breastbone facing down, and press down firmly with the heels of your hands to break the joints and flatten. Season with salt and pepper and brush with the olive oil and 2 tablespoons of the melted butter. Place skin-side up in a roasting pan in the oven and roast 35 to 40 minutes.

Remove the pan from the oven and heat the broiler to low. Drizzle the chicken evenly with the remaining melted butter, then brush with the mustard or wasabi, if using, and cover with the bread crumbs. Place under the broiler and broil 10 minutes, checking often to make sure the bread crumbs don't burn. Cut the chicken into 4 pieces and serve immediately with a chili oil dressing.

This is a great brasserie dish from the southwest of France, the foie gras region. There are so many varieties of duck to choose from; for this dish I recommend a corn-fed one, if possible, but definitely free range. For me this is hearty winter food, which is not to say it is too heavy for the summer: served with salad, it can make a terrific outdoor lunch. Whatever the season, you can't beat the flavor of crisp duck legs.

Confit de canard aux lentilles

DUCK CONFIT WITH LENTILS

Preparation time 40 minutes, plus making the vinaigrette and 6 to 8 hours marinating
Cooking time 3 to 4 hours

CONFIT

4 duck legs, about 6 ounces each, including fat

3 tablespoons sea salt

4 garlic cloves, unpeeled and crushed with the flat edge of a knife or your hand

4 thyme sprigs, leaves only

2¼ pounds goose or duck fat, melted

2 tablespoons honey

freshly ground black pepper

LENTILS

1 cup Puy lentils, picked over and rinsed

1 shallot

1 small carrot, peeled and diced

1 bouquet garni made with 1 thyme sprig and 1 parsley sprig, tied together with kitchen string

1 garlic clove, unpeeled

2 to 3 tablespoons French Vinaigrette (see page 20)

1 handful of chervil, leaves only, chopped

To make the duck leg confit, put the duck legs in a small roasting pan, skin-side down. Season with salt, pepper, garlic and thyme, cover with plastic wrap, press down and leave to marinate 2 to 3 hours in the refrigerator.

Heat the oven to 250°F. Take the duck out of the pan, discarding the marinade, then rinse under running cold water and dry on paper towels. Put the duck in a large Dutch oven and pour the melted goose fat on top. Cover with a lid or parchment paper sealed with foil, then place in the oven and cook 3 to 4 hours. Remove the Dutch oven from the oven, skim off any fat, cover with foil and set aside. Alternatively, you can gently simmer the duck on the hob, covered, 3 to 4 hours.

Meanwhile, make the lentils. Put them in a small saucepan and cover with cold water. Bring to a boil and skim the white foam from the surface. Add the whole shallot, carrot, bouquet garni and garlic, reduce the heat to low and simmer 10 minutes longer, or until al dente. Strain, reserving 2 tablespoons of the cooking liquid, and discard the shallot, bouquet garni and garlic, but leave the carrots in. Add the vinaigrette, the reserved cooking liquid and the chervil. Taste and adjust the seasoning with salt and pepper. This should give you a lovely salad.

Finally, brush the duck legs with the honey and pan-roast them, skin-side down, in a nonstick skillet over medium heat 5 minutes, or until crisp and golden brown. The honey will caramelize very quickly, so be careful not to let it burn.

Divide the lentils onto four plates, arrange the duck legs on top and enjoy! Alternatively, arrange in a large pot to serve from at the table. The texture and delicate flavors of this dish are second to none.

Les Trois-Épis is a high plateau on the Alsatian side of the Vosges mountains near Turckheim—it is surrounded by sweeping vineyards and has a stunning view of the valley below. Best known for the great Alsace wine it produces, it is also a hunting estate and became one of the favorite stomping grounds for my father and I whenever the hunting season arrived each year. A lesser known fact about Les Trois-Épis is that there are an unbelievable number of pheasants hiding among the vineyards eating grapes. When we started plucking pheasants at home as children, what struck us most was the color of the flesh—it was deep purple and smelled strongly of wine! The flavor was already so tremendous my mother didn't need much more than a few pieces of pancetta and some shallots to finish it off! She always preferred to roast pheasants in the pot, partly to retain the moisture, but also, I think, because she loved to lift the lid and smell the beautiful aroma. I can taste it like it was yesterday! Ah … those are the days I miss!

Faisan façon Maman

MAMAN'S POT-ROASTED PHEASANT

Preparation time 20 to 25 minutes, plus making the braised cabbage
Cooking time 1 hour 20 minutes

1 young pheasant, prepared by your butcher (including liver chopped and returned to the cavity)

2 slices of pancetta or smoked bacon

4 tablespoons sunflower oil

4 tablespoons butter

2 apples, peeled, cored and quartered

1 bouquet garni made with 1 thyme sprig and 1 parsley sprig, tied together with kitchen string

2 tablespoons brandy

1 cup heavy cream

sea salt and freshly ground black pepper

1 recipe quantity Braised Cabbage (see page 158) or vegetables of your choice, to serve

Take the pheasant, wrap the pancetta slices around the breast and use kitchen string to tie it all up—this holds everything together, keeping the pheasant breast moist.

Heat 2 tablespoons of the oil with the butter in a Dutch oven or cast-iron pot over medium heat, then add the pheasant and pot-roast, partially covered, 40 to 45 minutes until the meat is well sealed and almost cooked through. Turn the pheasant occasionally to make sure you get an even rich golden color all around. Remove the pheasant from the pot and set aside.

Reduce the heat to low and add the apples, bouquet garni and brandy. Stir the ingredients with a wooden spoon to lift any tasty bits that have stuck to the bottom of the pot. Return the pheasant to the pot. Partially cover and cook 10 minutes longer, then add the cream and simmer gently, uncovered, 25 minutes longer, or until the sauce reduces and is thick enough to coat the back of a spoon. Season with salt and pepper.

Serve the pheasant topped with the sauce and accompanied with braised cabbage or other vegetables of your choice.

In France, when we have the combination of truffles and potatoes in a dish, we talk about the rich mixing with the poor! Truffles can be expensive, but you don't need much and the addition transforms the simple into the spectacular. You can also freeze any you have left over. For this dish, you can also use a chicken, but I find guinea fowl has so much more texture and flavor. Originally a wild bird, it has since been domesticated—which I am glad about, otherwise people would really have missed out.

Blancs de pintade aux truffes et poireaux

PAN-ROASTED GUINEA FOWL WITH TRUFFLES & LEEKS

Preparation time 40 minutes
Cooking time 15 minutes

4 guinea fowl breast halves
  (or chicken if you prefer)

2 small black winter truffles, thinly
  sliced

3 tablespoons olive oil

1 leek or 3 baby leeks, green parts
  only, thinly sliced

2 cups small new potatoes cut into
  ¼-inch-thick slices

3 ounces pancetta, thinly sliced

2 chervil or flat-leaf parsley sprigs,
  roughly chopped

5 tablespoons butter

sea salt and freshly ground black
  pepper

Heat the oven to 350°F.

Slit the skin of the guinea fowl breast halves and place 3 thin slices of truffle underneath. Fold the skin back over the breast and season both sides of it with salt and pepper. Cut the remaining truffle slices into thin julienne strips and set aside for the vegetables. Heat 2 tablespoons of the oil in an ovenproof skillet over medium heat. Add the guinea fowl, skin-side down, and cook 2 to 3 minutes, until golden—make sure the pan is not too hot so the skin does not shrink back too much. Turn the guinea fowl over and cook a minute longer, then place in the oven 8 minutes. When ready, remove the breasts from the oven, put on a plate, set aside and keep warm.

While the guinea fowl is in the oven, heat two pans of salted water until boiling, then drop the leeks in one and cook 1 minute. Drain them, then refresh in ice-cold water and drain again. Put the potatoes into the other pan of boiling water and cook 6 minutes, then add the pancetta and cook 2 minutes longer. Drain them, then refresh in ice-cold water and drain again.

Heat a skillet over medium heat. Add the remaining olive oil, potatoes and pancetta and cook 1 to 2 minutes until golden brown. Add the leek, a pinch of the reserved truffle and the chervil to the skillet, then drain off any fat. Add 2 to 3 tablespoons water and stir to make a sauce. Add the butter and the remaining truffle and cook until the butter melts.

Cut each piece of guinea fowl in half lengthwise. Place some of the leek and potato mixture in the middle of each plate, put the guinea fowl on top and pour the truffle-and-butter sauce over.

All over France, hunters and cooks have for centuries prized wild rabbit for its lean meat and rich flavor. My grandparents kept rabbits on their farm, so I grew up eating farmed rabbit meat regularly. Although it was often overlooked in the last few decades, the meat is becoming popular again and farmed rabbit is now widely available. It tastes like chicken but with a more gamy flavor, and it's both delicious and nutritious. Even if you've never eaten rabbit before, give it a try. I'm sure you will enjoy it!

Lapin en cocotte au citron et à l'ail

RABBIT CASSEROLE WITH LEMON & GARLIC

Preparation time 20 minutes, plus marinating and making the stock and spinach
Cooking time 1 hour 10 minutes

juice and zest of 1 lemon

1 farmed rabbit, about 4½ pounds, cut into 8 pieces

6 tablespoons olive oil

1 tablespoon butter

4 garlic cloves, unpeeled and crushed with the flat edge of a knife or your hand

2 cups plus 2 tablespoons Chicken Stock (see page 18)

2 thyme or basil sprigs

sea salt and freshly ground black pepper

1 recipe quantity Buttered Spinach with Lemon Zest (see page 162), to serve

Heat the oven to 350°F. Put the lemon zest and juice in a large bowl, add the rabbit pieces and 2 tablespoons of the olive oil and season with salt and pepper. Leave to marinate 5 minutes.

Melt the butter and the remaining olive oil in a Dutch oven over medium heat and sauté the rabbit pieces until golden brown, 8 to 10 minutes on each side. (You might have to do this in 2 batches, depending on the size of your pot.) Add the garlic and the lemon marinade to the pot and stir to deglaze—there will be a bit of a splash and some smoke. Leave the liquid to reduce about 5 minutes until it is slightly syrupy and coats the back of a spoon. You will be able to tell when it's ready if when you run 2 fingers down the back of the spoon the 2 lines don't immediately join. Add the stock and thyme. Bring to a boil, then transfer the Dutch oven to the oven and cook 30 to 35 minutes.

Transfer the rabbit from the Dutch oven to an ovenproof serving dish and keep warm in the oven. Return the Dutch oven to the stovetop and bring the cooking liquid to a boil, then reduce the heat to low and simmer, uncovered, 3 to 5 minutes until it has the consistency of a light syrup.

Pour the sauce over the rabbit and serve with buttered spinach.

This is a dish that used to be on the table very often during the hunting season, as Papa went shooting twice a week. He was a very good shot and loved it, so we always had game to eat and a full freezer for the rest of the year. Preparing this dish was very much Maman's domain and specialty, but I used to help a lot and really enjoyed preparing the vegetables for the roast to come. This is a simple dish, but it requires attention to get it right and you need young game for tenderness. This version is only rubbed quickly with oil and sea salt and is missing a classic red wine marinade, which, generally, I would reserve for older game, or *grand veneur.*

Cuisse de chevreuil en cocotte

VENISON CASSEROLE

Preparation time 40 minutes
Cooking time 1 hour 20 minutes

2 tablespoons sea salt

4 tablespoons sunflower oil

1 venison haunch, about 4 pounds, tied up with string

2 carrots, peeled and cut in half, then cut in half lengthwise

2 shallots, peeled and cut into small pieces lengthwise

1 small head of garlic, unpeeled and cut in half horizontally

1 large thyme sprig

2 tablespoons brandy

3 tablespoons butter

freshly ground black pepper

cooked chestnuts, to serve

Rub the sea salt and 2 tablespoons of the oil all over the venison.

Heat the remaining oil in a large Dutch oven over medium heat and fry the venison 15 to 18 minutes, turning constantly, until golden brown all around. Season with pepper, then add the carrots and shallots and continue cooking, partially covered to reduce the condensation. Lower the heat slightly so it does not burn.

After the venison has cooked 30 minutes, stir in the garlic and thyme, then add the brandy to deglaze and flambé. To do this, light a match and incline the pan slightly at an angle away from you so the flames take hold. (Make sure there are no children around.) Alternatively, let the liquid reduce by half during the cooking process by removing the lid.

Continue cooking the venison 20 minutes longer, uncovered if reducing the liquid now and checking regularly to make sure it stays nice and moist. If the venison starts to dry, partially re-cover the pot to retain some of the moisture. Remove the meat from the Dutch oven, transfer it to a warm serving dish, set aside and keep warm.

You should have some lovely juice at the bottom of the Dutch oven and your vegetables should be golden and almost glazed. Add the butter to them and stir until combined, then season with salt and pepper. Keep warm while you carve the venison.

Pour the sauce, what we call "jus" in a professional kitchen, over the venison and serve with the vegetables and chestnuts.

Filets de carrelet meunière aux amandes

Filets de bar aux citrons caramelisés

Sole au beurre citronné et persil

Bar en croûte de sel avec salade d'endives à l'orange

Moules marinières à la citronnelle et au piment

Gambas sautées au beurre d'ail et piment

Bouillabaisse

Les Poissons et Les Fruits de Mer

FISH & SHELLFISH

If you wander the coastal cities of France, you will stumble upon brasseries with some spectacular seafood. At the entrance you will probably see display tables of freshly caught fish and shellfish laid out on ice, and inside you might find a tank with live lobsters and crabs, ready to be chosen and cooked *à la minute*. When seafood is this fresh you don't need to do much with it—simply broiling or roasting and a little herb butter, such as Dover Sole with Lemon & Parsley Butter, is all it needs. When eating at home with family or friends, we often enjoy delicious all-in-one pots of seafood, such as a Bouillabaisse or Moules Marinières with Lemongrass & Chili—there's nothing quite like it.

Unlike most freshwater fish, salmon have the ability to move freely between rivers and oceans because their bodies can adjust to changes in salt content. When it's time to lay their eggs and let the cycle begin again—and they always know when it is—salmon make the treacherous journey home, swimming upstream, navigating their way over rocks and through waterfalls, dodging predators, traveling hundreds of miles to return to the exact place they were born. When I teach trainees, I often talk about how important it is to treat your ingredients with respect. In the salmon's case, I think they've earned it!

Steak de saumon poêlé avec mayonnaise au citron vert et coriandre

PAN-ROASTED SALMON STEAKS WITH LIME & CILANTRO MAYONNAISE

Preparation time 15 minutes, plus making the potatoes
Cooking time 10 minutes

4 skinless salmon steaks, about 5 ounces each

2 tablespoons olive oil

1 tablespoon butter

sea salt and freshly ground black pepper

1 recipe quantity Warm Crushed Potatoes with Cilantro & Lime (see page 163), to serve

LIME & CILANTRO MAYONNAISE

7 tablespoons mayonnaise

1 small handful of cilantro, leaves only, chopped

zest of 1 lime, plus extra for sprinkling

juice of ½ lime

To make the cilantro and lime mayonnaise, put the mayonnaise, cilantro leaves and lime zest and juice in a small bowl. Season with salt and pepper and mix to combine. This gives the mayonnaise a deliciously light zing and makes the dish really colorful.

For the pan-roasted salmon, season the salmon steaks with salt and pepper. Heat the olive oil and butter in a large skillet over medium heat. When the butter is starting to foam, add the salmon steaks and cook 4 to 5 minutes on each side until light golden.

Put the salmon steaks on four plates, top with the mayonnaise, sprinkle with extra lime zest and serve immediately with warm crushed potatoes.

CHEF'S TIP: *Instead of pan-roasting the salmon, you can poach it. To do this, place a saucepan of salted water over medium-high heat and bring to a boil, then throw in a few sprigs of cilantro and a peeled and crushed garlic clove. Reduce the heat to low, add the salmon and poach 5 minutes, or until it flakes off the fork and is still slightly pink in the middle, then drain and serve. This is a delicious and very healthy alternative to pan-roasting.*

Summer is the best time of the year to enjoy Dover sole, but the similarly named but unrelated lemon sole is more widely available —you can find it during most of the year—which means you can enjoy this dish all year round, too. For me, sole is sublime: elegant, firm and deliciously delicate, yet full of flavor. Although it is very versatile, sole actually needs nothing more than broiling and topping with a light, hazelnut-colored herb butter to create perfection—pure and simple! This dish is delicious served with new potatoes and buttered spinach.

Sole au beurre citronné et persil

DOVER SOLE WITH LEMON & PARSLEY BUTTER

Preparation time 10 minutes
Cooking time 12 minutes

4 skinless Dover sole or lemon sole
   fillets, about 5 ounces each

1 tablespoon all-purpose flour

2 tablespoons olive oil

½ cup butter, softened

juice and zest of 1 lemon

1 handful of flat-leaf parsley, leaves
   only, chopped

sea salt and freshly ground black
   pepper

Heat the oven to 400°F and heat a grill pan (ideally cast iron) or heavy-bottomed skillet over medium heat.

Pat the sole dry with paper towels, then put it in a shallow dish and dust lightly with the flour. When the pan is hot, place the fillets on it, one at a time, and cook 1 minute. Rotate the fish 90 degrees and cook 1 minute longer to create a crisscross pattern.

Drizzle a heavy-bottomed roasting pan with the olive oil. Arrange the sole on the tray, cooked side up, then place one-quarter of the butter on each, season with salt and pepper and finish cooking in the oven 3 to 4 minutes until golden brown. Remove the fish from the pan, set aside and keep warm.

When the fish is cooked, add the lemon juice and zest and parsley to the pan and combine with the butter. Divide the fish onto four plates, spoon the parsley butter over the tops and serve.

When you are traveling through France, this fish can be rather confusing. In the North it is called *bar* and in the South *loup de mer*, meaning "wolf of the sea"—probably due to the sea bass' voracity and its habit of hunting in groups. It is widely available, because it is farmed, but can still be a little pricey. One farmed fish, however, happily feeds at least two people. This recipe harmonizes the sweet acidity of caramelized lemon with the grassiness of basil oil—I think it might be one of my favorites.

Filets de bar aux citrons caramelisés

FILLET OF SEA BASS WITH CARAMELIZED LEMONS

Preparation time 25 minutes, plus making the potatoes
Cooking time 20 minutes

2 lemons, thinly sliced

6 tablespoons olive oil

1 small handful of basil

2 teaspoons confectioners' sugar

4 sea bass fillets, about 5 ounces each, skins on

12 cherry tomatoes

basil-infused olive oil, for drizzling

sea salt and freshly ground black pepper

1 recipe quantity Sautéed Potatoes with Parsley & Garlic (see page 163), to serve

Heat the oven to 350°F. Put the lemon slices on a baking sheet, season with salt and pepper and drizzle 2 tablespoons of the olive oil over. Cover with the basil leaves and leave to marinate 5 minutes.

Heat a cast-iron grill pan, or heavy-bottomed skillet, over medium heat. Dust the lemon slices on one side only with confectioners' sugar and place them on the pan, sugar side down. Cook 1 to 2 minutes until caramelized and golden, being careful not to burn the lemon—lower the heat, if necessary, because the sugar will color quickly. Transfer to a baking dish and set aside.

Season the fish with salt and pepper, drizzle with 2 tablespoons of the remaining olive oil and put on the grill pan, skin-side down. Cook 1 minute, then rotate the fillets 90 degrees and cook 1 minute longer on the same side to create a crisscross pattern.

Put the fish on top of the lemon, then add the cherry tomatoes to the dish and season with salt and pepper. Drizzle with the remaining olive oil and finish cooking 8 minutes until the skin is slighty crisp and the flesh is white and still moist when tested with the tines of a fork.

Serve the sea bass sprinkled with the basil oil and accompanied with sautéed potatoes.

This is a typical brasserie dish found all over France and can be made with either sea bass, porgy or sea bream. When baking in a sea salt crust, it is always best to cook the whole fish rather than fillets, because it makes the flavor so much better. It is slightly less practical, because you have to pick out the bones afterward—but what you lose in convenience you gain in flavor. The combination of the fish with the endive and citrus salad makes this a light, refreshing dish that zings! And don't worry about the salt content—it's just a casing to bring out the flavor.

Bar en croûte de sel avec salade d'endives à l'orange

SEA BASS BAKED IN SEA SALT WITH BELGIAN ENDIVE & ORANGE SALAD

Preparation time 30 minutes
Cooking time 15 minutes

2 egg whites

juice and zest of ½ lime

zest of ½ orange

4 pounds rock sea salt

1 whole sea bass, about 3 pounds, drawn

olive oil, for drizzling

sea salt and freshly ground black pepper

BELGIAN ENDIVE & ORANGE SALAD

1 orange (ideally a blood orange, if available)

2 heads of Belgian endives

2 heads of radicchio

½ small handful of dill, roughly chopped

2 tablespoons olive oil

½ tablespoon reduced balsamic vinegar

Heat the oven to 375°F. Put the egg whites in a large mixing bowl and whisk until stiff peaks form. Add a squeeze of lime juice, the lime and orange zests and the salt and mix by hand, or with a spatula if you prefer. Line a roasting pan with waxed paper and spoon over one-quarter of the salt mixture in a layer. Place the sea bass on the salt, then cover it completely with the remaining salt mix, pressing the salt down firmly around the fish.

Bake the fish 15 minutes, then remove the pan from the oven and leave the fish to rest for 2 minutes without touching the salt crust.

Meanwhile, prepare the salad. Grate the orange zest and set aside, then peel the orange and cut the segments from between the membrane. Do this over a bowl to catch the juices, adding the segments to the bowl.

Cut off the bottom and outer leaves of the Belgian endive and radicchio, then cut each head in half, lengthwise, and remove the core. Put the leaves in a separate bowl. Add the orange zest, dill and oil and mix until combined. Just before serving, add the reduced balsamic vinegar, 2 tablespoons of the reserved orange juice and half the orange segments. (Adding the acidic ingredients at the last minute is essential to keep the salad fresh and crunchy.) Season with pepper and whisk until well combined.

To serve, break the top of the salt crust by knocking it gently with a wooden spoon. Remove the skin from the fish (it might come off with the crust). Lift the top fillet of fish off the bone with a fork and put it on a warm serving plate (one fillet should be enough for 2 people). Remove the bone from the fish, revealing the second fillet underneath, then transfer it to the serving plate. Drizzle with oil and season with salt and pepper. Serve immediately with the salad for a light, fresh and colorful dish.

In England, I often cook sea bream for demos at food festivals and on TV because I think it is underrated and isn't a fish people necessarily think of eating at home. This is a great pity, because it has lovely white flesh, a firm texture similar to that of sea bass and is perfect for steaming, broiling, baking and frying— in fact, for most types of Mediterranean cooking. Porgy is the American variety of sea bream and is available most of the year, so why not give it a try? I think you'll be pleasantly surprised.

Filets de daurade, ragoût de pommes de terre et oignons avec sauce vierge

FILLETS OF PORGY WITH POTATO & SCALLION RAGOUT & SAUCE VIERGE

Preparation time 15 minutes, plus making the sauce
Cooking time 30 minutes

12 small new potatoes

1 small fennel bulb

scant 1 cup pancetta cut into ¼-inch-thin strips

4 porgy or sea bream fillets, 5 ounces each, scaled and pin-boned but skin on

1 tablespoon olive oil

1 bunch of scallions, finely sliced

sea salt and freshly ground black pepper

1 recipe quantity Sauce Vierge (see page 21), kept warm, to serve

Heat the oven to 350°F. Bring a large saucepan of salted water to a boil and cook the potatoes and fennel over medium-low heat 15 minutes. The potatoes should still be firm, because you will sauté them later. Drain and peel the potatoes, then cut them into thick slices and set aside. Discard the fennel.

Bring another saucepan of water to a boil and blanch the pancetta 30 seconds to remove the excess salt. Refresh in cold water, then drain and set aside on paper towels.

Season the porgy fillets with salt and pepper. Heat a heavy-bottomed skillet over medium heat and cook the fillets, skin-side down, 4 minutes, or until the skins start to turn crisp. Transfer the fish to a baking sheet, skin side down, then place in the oven and roast 6 minutes, or until the flesh is white but still moist.

Meanwhile, make the ragout. Heat the olive oil in a skillet over medium heat. Add the potatoes and pancetta and cook 5 minutes, or until the potatoes are starting to turn golden. Add the scallions and sauté 2 minutes longer. Be careful not to break up the potatoes. Gently warm the sauce vierge while making the ragout.

Divide the potato and scallion ragout onto four plates, arrange a fillet of fish on top of each, drizzle with the sauce and serve.

If you are using large red mullet, you will need to ask your fish merchant to scale and draw them, but with the smaller ones drawing is not necessary because they have nothing inside except the liver. If you were a French fisherman, you would probably just scale them in the sea water and cook them on board with a camping stove. If you are at home, it is not so different—simply pan-fry them with garlic, thyme and a squeeze of lemon. Lovely! Red mullet is popular all along the Mediterranean and I urge you to try it when you have the chance. If you can't source any, try this recipe with whole porgy or filleted ocean perch. Just be sure to ask your fish merchant to scale the fish for you.

Rouget petit bateau poêlé au thym

PAN-FRIED RED MULLET WITH THYME

Preparation time 20 minutes, plus
making the potatoes
Cooking time 15 minutes

4 garlic cloves, unpeeled

1 tablespoon olive oil

4 whole red mullet or porgy, about 6 ounces each, scaled and drawn but with skins left on, or 8 fillets red mullet or ocean perch, scaled but with skins left on

2 tablespoons butter

1 handful of thyme sprigs

juice of ½ lemon

sea salt and freshly ground black pepper

1 recipe quantity Warm Crushed Potatoes with Cilantro & Lime (see page 163), to serve

Heat the oven to 350°F. Bring a saucepan of water to a boil and blanch the garlic 3 to 4 minutes. This will make sure it cooks in the same time as the fish. Drain the garlic and pat dry with paper towels.

If using whole fish, heat the olive oil in a large, heavy-bottomed skillet over medium heat. Season the whole fish with salt and pepper, then add them and the garlic to the pan. Cook 2 minutes, or until the skin is a lovely golden color. Turn the fish over, add the butter and thyme and cook 2 minutes longer. Transfer to a small roasting pan and place in the oven 3 to 4 minutes until the flesh starts to break up. Remove the pan from the oven, drizzle the fish with the lemon juice and season with salt and pepper.

If using fillets, heat the olive oil in large, heavy-bottomed skillet over medium heat. Season the fish with salt and pepper, then add to the pan, skin side down, along with the garlic, butter and thyme. Cook 2 minutes, or until the skin is a lovely golden color. Transfer the fillets to a baking sheet and place it in the oven 2 minutes, or until the flesh starts to break up. Remove the baking sheet from the oven, drizzle the fish with the lemon juice and season with salt and pepper, then serve.

Serve 1 whole fish or 2 fillets per person with warm crushed potatoes. Be sure to include a garlic clove with each portion—just squeeze the tender flesh out of the skin on the side of your plate to enjoy with the fish.

Les Poissons et Les Fruits de Mer
Fish & Shellfish

The topic of fish and shellfish is almost as vast as the sea itself, and one that I have a particular love for. It is my favorite subject and section in the kitchen. My brother Patrick and I used to go fishing in the river when we were young. We'd pack a *casse-croûte*, or snack, along with worms or bread for bait, and set off early in the morning, often to the same spot. We were fishing for *perche soleil*, a fish named for its rainbowlike color. Sometimes we were lucky, sometimes not, but we always enjoyed the peace and quiet of a misty morning and the chance to chat. Patrick was always with me, good company and very funny. Most of the time we came back empty-handed or with just a few spiny-finned fish, enough only for a small fried dish, but we were always happy to have spent some time together.

When learning my trade, I went to Brittany for a summer season. I was very young, maybe 16 or 17, and I recall the restaurant was in a small fishing village called Raguenes, right on the beach. When I think back, I know this is where my love for fish and shellfish comes from. Sometimes I went with the owner of the restaurant to a very small island called Île Verte to drop lobster traps. It was a prime spot for a great catch, and one that was passed on to him by his father. A few days later, we went back and pulled up the traps, then cooked the lobster according to the family recipe. I have kept that recipe well under wraps ever since and only ever cook lobster that way at home. It is delicious.

Every morning, local fishermen would come to the door with a massive quantity of fish, the quality of which was unbelievable. One of the most popular was sea bass, a very meaty fish with firm flesh, which is equally delicious whether broiled, pan-fried, braised or roasted. Versatile and tasty, they are available all year round, although it's best to avoid them in March to June when they are spawning. Other favorites were sardines, a nutritious oily fish, which we broiled

or barbecued whole, or made into *bouillabaisse*; and ling, which are perfect in a fish pie. These days they are much in demand and, therefore, overfished, so I only buy them if they are line-caught and have them occasionally as a treat.

The sustainability of fish is a big issue these days and one that we all need to consider. In my restaurant we try to make sure that we buy from a sustainable source. It is very important we find the right suppliers who provide us with the best possible fish that is also sourced from sustainable stocks. It is too easy to forget most species are overfished, and, therefore, becoming not only expensive but increasingly rare. So, for example, whenever possible we buy hand-dived scallops, not dredged ones; line-caught fish, not net-caught; and farmed, but organically reared fish.

Of course, I want my son's generation to be able to enjoy eating fish not only now but in the future. That is why it is important for us to protect our fish stocks and also learn to respect the product. In my kitchen, we try to do just that by teaching our staff how to scale, draw and cut a fish properly and how to prepare shellfish. Too often, you buy fish and shellfish that are badly damaged by not having been handled properly. But I love going to the fish merchant and seeing the eye-catching display of fish that shows the rightful care it was given. The colorful line-up, the shine and the presence—it is beautiful, and you know you will enjoy preparing, cooking and eating the fish you buy there.

I can't stress enough how necessary it is to buy fresh, quality produce from a good source. A fish should be firm to the touch and its skin and eyes should look bright—dullness or discoloration denote it is past its best. And smell it, too. A fresh fish has a "clean," not overly "fishy" odor, and sea fish often smell slightly salty or like seaweed. Lobsters and crabs should look undamaged and feel heavy for their size, while all shellfish should have tightly closed shells.

In my restaurant, I go around the tables to talk to my customers and often, when I discuss fish with them, they say they don't like it because they had bad experiences with it in the past. If this sounds like you, I encourage you to try again. I have challenged and, I hope, changed many people's negative attitudes toward fish and shellfish over the years. If you buy fresh fish or shellfish, prepare it in the correct way and follow one of the recipes in this book, I bet you will experience great pleasure from eating it! Before you know it you will be eating fish regularly, which is great for your health— it's a great source of many nutrients, especially oily fish, which contain brain-boosting omega-3 fatty acids. At home we have fish as often as possible. I prefer it to meat anytime! Well… except, perhaps, for a Sunday roast.

I've included a lot of fish recipes in this book, all different and all, I hope, interesting. Some I have created myself over the years; others I've eaten or found elsewhere and they have inspired me to make my own version. The recipes are drawn from all over France and show you many ways of cooking fish and shellfish. From classic Dover sole, roasted porgy and traditional bouillabaisse to mussels, scallops, clams, crabs, langoustines, flounder, salmon, monkfish, John Dory, jumbo shrimp, anchovies and many more, they are all here—a veritable feast from the sea!

You will probably already be familiar with some of the fish I include in my recipes, such as the beautiful mackerel with its blue-black stripes, full of omega-3 fatty acids and packed with goodness. It is delicious broiled, smoked, pan-roasted, whole or in fillet form. You will also know tuna, which I really like. I adore blue-fin tuna, but as this fish is very rare I only buy it farmed; instead, I have yellow-fin or skipjack. I love tuna raw, pan-fried or marinated, and eat it often as it is available all year

round. Other fish you will probably be acquainted with are haddock and hake. Haddock belongs to the cod family, but is smaller than cod. The flesh is white and delicate and it is usually sold as a whole fish or in fillets. Like cod, it has been overfished, so to help protect the stocks, it's best to have it only occasionally. Hake has lovely white flesh and is very good in *gratin* dishes or pan-fried with butter sauces.

I hope you will discover some new fish among the recipes in this book, too, such as pollack, which is now becoming a popular alternative to or substitute for cod and haddock. Found in the North Atlantic, this fish has a fine texture and can be cooked as steaks, deep-fried, baked *en papillotte* or prepared like salt cod. It can be found all year round. but is best avoided in January to April, when it is spawning. Black bream is increasingly available. Its soft, white, dense flesh is succulent. I love it broiled or grilled whole or baked in sea salt. And, what about turbot? This flatfish lives on the sandy, pebbly beds of the Atlantic Ocean, with the best quality imported from Europe; it is usually sold frozen in the United States. It has beautiful white, transparent flesh and is very firm to the touch. It is an expensive fish, so it is great for special occasions. Very versatile, turbot can be poached, roasted, steamed or pan-fried. Again, buy farmed or line-caught turbot whenever possible, or use its cousin brill, which is less under threat.

Lastly, I'd very much like you to try red mullet whenever you have the opportunity. I know its not often available in the States, but it is very popular in France and possibly my favorite fish of all. It's very delicate, has a strong "sea rock" flavor, firm flesh and is a beautiful light pink color. (You can substitute porgy in any recipe for whole red mullet or ocean perch for the fillets.) It can be baked, shallow-fried or cooked *en papillote*, but some of the best red mullet I've tasted has been simply broiled or pan-fried. Delicious!

left page from top: red gunard (rockfish),
mackerel, jumbo shrimp, sea bass,
red mullet, pollack

right page from top: flounder, John Dory,
sardines, black bream, langoustines

One of the best-known and loved flatfish of all, flounder can be easily identified at the fish merchant's by its distinctive brown coloring and vivid orange spots. If cooked well, this tasty fish can be every bit as good as Dover sole, and it is a much cheaper alternative, too. This recipe helps to bring out the natural meatiness of the fish and is one found on brasserie menus across France, perhaps not always with almonds, but certainly *à la meunière*. Who can resist it?

Filets de carrelet meunière aux amandes

PAN-FRIED FILLET OF FLOUNDER WITH BUTTER & ALMONDS

Preparation time 15 minutes
Cooking time 15 minutes

4 flounder fillets, about 4 ounces each

2 tablespoons all-purpose flour

4 tablespoons butter

2 tablespoons olive oil

¼ cup slivered almonds

1 handful of flat-leaf parsley, leaves only, finely chopped

juice of ½ lemon

sea salt and freshly ground black pepper

Put the fillets on a cutting board, season with salt and pepper and sprinkle with flour. Pat them briefly with paper towels to remove any excess flour, so there is just a fine dusting left on the fish.

Melt half the butter with the olive oil in a large, heavy-bottomed skillet over medium-low heat. When the butter begins to foam, add the fillets and cook 4 to 5 minutes on each side until they are a lovely golden color and firm to the touch. Put the fillets on a plate, set aside and keep warm while you finish the butter sauce.

Add the remaining butter and the slivered almonds to the pan and cook until they are just golden. Throw in the parsley, add the lemon juice and season with salt and pepper.

Divide the fillets onto four plates, then pour the nutty, buttery sauce over and serve immediately .

At home, I cook a lot of fish *en papillotte* because it is quick, easy and full of flavor, a good everyday option. *En papillotte* simply means "cooked in packages," so all the flavor and goodness are locked inside. When you open up the package, you release a rush of aromas that take you on a journey without ever leaving your kitchen. You can make so many variations of this dish: ginger and lemongrass, chili and cilantro, lemon and basil, or lime and parsley. Experiment—you won't be disappointed.

Filets de morue en papillotte à la coriandre, ail et tomate

COD, CILANTRO, TOMATO & GARLIC PACKAGES

Preparation time 20 minutes, plus making the rice
Cooking time 20 minutes

4 skinless, boneless cod fillets, about 5 ounces each

4 garlic cloves, unpeeled

4 tablespoons olive oil

2 large tomatoes, sliced

1 small handful of cilantro, leaves only, chopped

sea salt and freshly ground black pepper

steamed or boiled rice mixed with a handful of chopped cilantro leaves, to serve

Heat the oven to 400°F and bring a small saucepan of lightly salted water to a boil. Pat the fish dry with paper towels, season with salt and set aside.

Blanch the garlic in the boiling water 2 minutes, then refresh in cold water and pat dry. That way it will cook in the same time as the fish once it is *en papillotte*.

Put four 18- x 10-inch rectangles of parchment paper on your countertop and drizzle them with half the olive oil. Next, you need to arrange the ingredients on one half of the paper, so you will be able to fold the other half of the paper over them afterward. Start with a few slices of tomato on each piece of foil and divide half the cilantro over them, then season with salt and pepper. Put the pieces of cod on top of the tomatoes, then add the blanched garlic and the rest of the cilantro and drizzle with the remaining olive oil. Fold the paper over the filling and then fold along the edges to seal securely. Make sure the packages are well sealed so none of the juices are lost during cooking. Put the packages on a baking sheet and bake 15 minutes. Remove the tray from the oven and let the fish rest 2 minutes before opening the packages.

Now comes the rush of aromas—open each package, taking care not to lose any of the juices, and serve with cilantro-scented rice. Squeeze the tender garlic out of its skin for an extra delicious flavor.

CHEF'S TIP: *If sustainable cod is not available, use pollack fillets instead.*

When a dish has olives in it, more often than not it comes from the South of France. I love olives, so it follows I love the food from the south, and I couldn't resist including this recipe. It's a great classic from Nice and a firm favorite on brasserie menus everywhere. As an alternative, for something a little different, it can also be made with artichokes and fava beans. Either way, it's full of exhilarating fresh flavors and vibrant color.

Salade niçoise

NIÇOISE SALAD

Preparation time 30 minutes
Cooking time 55 minutes

1 red bell pepper

11 ounces small new potatoes

7 ounces green beans, trimmed

4 eggs or 8 quail eggs

4 tomatoes, cut into wedges

1 white or red onion, sliced into thin rings

⅔ cup pitted black olives, or green if preferred

3 ounces anchovies in oil, drained

9 ounces fresh tuna steaks (from a sustainable source)

sea salt and freshly ground black pepper

DRESSING

1 large shallot, finely chopped

2 garlic cloves, finely sliced

6 tablespoons olive oil, plus extra for frying

2 tablespoons red wine vinegar

Heat the oven to 400°F, then roast the whole bell pepper 30 minutes. Remove it from the oven and place it in a bowl. Cover the bowl with plastic wrap and set aside until the pepper cools.

Bring three saucepans of salted water to a boil. In one pan, cook the potatoes 15 to 20 minutes until tender and you can easily push a sharp knife through them. Drain them and set aside until they are cool enough to handle.

Meanwhile, cook the green beans 10 minutes in the second pan, then refresh under cold running water so they keep their form and color. In the third pan, hard-boil the eggs 8 minutes or quail eggs 4 minutes, then drain and leave to cool.

To make the dressing, whisk the shallot, garlic, oil and vinegar together in a small bowl. Season with salt and pepper and set aside.

Peel, seed and slice the pepper lengthwise. Peel the potatoes and cut them into thick slices, then peel the eggs and cut into quarters. (If using quail eggs, cut them in half only.) Arrange the peppers, tomatoes, onion and eggs on a large, deep platter and top with the olives and anchovies.

Season the tuna with salt and pepper. Heat a large skillet over medium heat. Add a little olive oil, then add the tuna and cook 1 to 2 minutes on each side until brown on the outside but still rare in the middle. Put the tuna on top of the salad, pour the dressing over and serve.

Saffron is one of the most expensive and treasured spices in the world. It takes about 4,300 crocus flowers to produce just one ounce saffron, and the threadlike stigmas are hand-picked. Fortunately, its intensity of flavor and color mean that the smallest amount brings an incredible aroma and flavor to this dish.

Pavé de lotte rôtie, ragoût de moules et palourdes au safran

ROAST MONKFISH FILLET WITH SAFFRON-SCENTED MUSSEL & CLAM RAGOUT

Preparation time 35 minutes, plus cooking the rice and asparagus
Cooking time 30 minutes

1 monkfish fillet, about 14 ounces, skinned and boned

14 ounces fresh mussels

7 ounces fresh clams

2 tablespoons olive oil

4 tablespoons butter

1 shallot, finely chopped

a pinch of saffron threads

7 tablespoons heavy cream, half of it whipped

zest of 1 lime

1 small handful of chives, roughly snipped

sea salt and freshly ground black pepper

steamed rice, to serve

cooked asparagus, to serve

Heat the oven to 400°F. Wrap the monkfish in a clean dish towel and set aside. This will absorb excess liquid and make it easier to roast.

Remove and discard the beards from the mussels and wash them and the clams in a bowl under running cold water, scrubbing well to remove all traces of grit. Discard any that float or any open ones that do not close when tapped. Set aside.

Put half the oil and butter in a skillet with an ovenproof handle over medium heat. When the butter begins to foam, add the monkfish and cook 4 to 5 minutes, turning continuously, until it has a lovely golden color all over. Transfer the skillet to the oven and roast the monkfish 8 minutes, or until firm to the touch. Remove the skillet from the oven, transfer the monkfish to a clean dish, cover with aluminum foil and set aside.

Put the remaining oil and butter in a Dutch oven over medium heat. When the butter is foaming, add the shallot and cook 1 minute, stirring, then add the mussels, clams and saffron. Cover and cook 4 to 5 minutes until the shellfish open. Discard any mussels or clams that remain closed.

Pour the unwhipped cream into the pan with the shellfish and cook, uncovered, over medium to high heat, 2 minutes. Remove the pan from the heat, use a slotted spoon to transfer the shellfish to a large bowl, then cover and set aside. Return the pan with the cooking liquid to medium heat and simmer 4 to 5 minutes until it reduces by half. Stir in the whipped cream and cook 2 to 3 minutes longer.

Remove the pan from the heat, add the lime zest, chives and any juices that have collected from the monkfish and season with salt and pepper. You should now have about ½ cup sauce.

Slice the monkfish into 4 pieces and either divide onto four plates with the ragout and a few spoonfuls of the sauce spooned over, or serve from the Dutch oven at the table with steamed rice and asparagus alongside.

Bouillabaisse, an elaborate fish soup from Marseilles in the South of France, is the very essence of the sea. Originally the food of poor fishermen, who put in it whatever they hadn't been able to sell that day, it has evolved into a voluptuous mix of succulent fish and shellfish, made enticing with herbs, spices and vegetables.

Bouillabaisse

BOUILLABAISSE

Preparation time 20 minutes
Cooking time 55 minutes

4 tablespoons olive oil

1 large onion, chopped

1 leek, thinly sliced and rinsed

1 fennel bulb, chopped

3 tomatoes, peeled and chopped

2 tablespoons tomato paste

4 garlic cloves, peeled and crushed
   with the flat edge of a knife or
   your hand

1 thyme sprig

a large pinch of saffron threads

4 pounds fish and shellfish such as
   follows:
   4 large langoustines or jumbo
      shrimp, crushed with a rolling pin
   2 rascasse, mullet or black bream,
      scaled, drawn and dressed
   2 John Dory or lemon sole, scaled,
      drawn, dressed and cut into
      portions
   4 slices of hake, pollack or haddock
   4 small red bream, scaled, drawn
      and dressed

4 tablespoons white wine

2 tablespoons aniseed-flavored liquor,
   such as Pastis or Pernod

1 handful of flat-leaf parsley, leaves
   only, roughly chopped

sea salt and freshly ground black
   pepper

crusty farmhouse bread, to serve

Heat a little of the oil in a large Dutch oven over medium heat and cook the onion, leek and fennel 4 to 5 minutes, stirring occasionally. Add the tomatoes, tomato paste, garlic, thyme and saffron and cook 2 minutes longer, stirring occasionally. Add the langoustines and stir until they are a deep orange color. Add the wine and liqueur and stir to deglaze. Add 4 cups water and cook a good 30 minutes, by which time the soup will already have a great flavor and rich color. Strain and press the mixture through a colander into a clean saucepan that is large enough to hold all the fish you are about to add. Discard anything that remains of the langoustines.

Return the soup to medium heat, add all the fish, except the red bream, and cook 7 to 8 minutes. Add the red bream and cook 6 minutes longer, then season with salt and pepper. Remove the pot from the heat, stir in the parsley and serve hot with crusty farmhouse bread.

CHEF'S TIPS: *Ask your fish merchant to prepare all the fish for you—don't be shy, that is what he or she is there for. Get him or her to scale, draw and dress whatever you like, and to cut the big fish into portions, except for the red bream and the langoustines, which should be kept whole.*

If you want to make it a hearty and more complete meal, add 3 cups peeled potatoes cut into large cubes to the fish bouillon when you add the first batch of fish—they will soak up all the goodness, too.

Scallops are sublime—I don't think I know anyone who doesn't like them. If you live near a harbor and can get hold of hand-dived, day-boat scallops, then snap them up! When scallops are dredged, they are usually full of sand or mud, which has an enormous effect on their flavor, but if they are hand-dived you won't have that problem. You can prepare this recipe by simply roasting the scallops, but they are much tastier cooked in the shell—and this is a fun way to serve them, too.

Noix de Saint-Jacques au beurre de curry et herbes

SCALLOPS WITH CURRY & HERB BUTTER

Preparation time 15 minutes
Cooking time 6 minutes

16 large scallops in their shells, trimmed by the fish merchant

1 teaspoon mild curry powder

2 small garlic cloves, finely chopped

1½ handfuls of chervil, finely chopped

1½ handfuls of chives, finely snipped

¾ cup plus 2 tablespoons butter, softened

juice of 1 lemon

sea salt and freshly ground black pepper

cooked asparagus, to serve (optional)

baguette, to serve (optional)

Heat the broiler to medium.

Season the scallops with salt and pepper and a light dusting of curry powder, then put them on a baking sheet.

Put the garlic, chervil, chives and butter in a bowl and mix together. Divide the mixture between the scallops, then place the tray under the broiler and broil 5 to 6 minutes until the butter is golden brown. Squeeze a few drops of lemon over each scallop.

Serve immediately. These are delicious with asparagus and fresh baguette.

Whether broiled, sautéed, pan-roasted or cooked in a bouillon, jumbo shrimp are quick, easy and delicious. In brasseries all over France, they are taken fresh from the tank and sautéed with sea salt. When cooking at home, you will need to buy them shelled from your fish merchant (make sure they're deveined, too). Try to avoid frozen shrimp if you can—as always with seafood, it is not worth compromising on the freshness.

Gambas sautées au beurre d'ail et piment

SAUTÉED JUMBO SHRIMP WITH CHILI & GARLIC BUTTER

Preparation time 10 minutes
Cooking time 6 minutes

8 jumbo or 24 small raw shrimp, shelled and deveined

2 tablespoons olive oil

6 tablespoons butter

1 red chili, seeded and finely chopped

2 garlic cloves, crushed with the flat edge of a knife or your hand and finely chopped

1 small handful of flat-leaf parsley, leaves only, finely chopped

juice and zest of 1 lime

salt and freshly ground black pepper

Wash the shrimp and dry them on paper towels. Warm the oil and 2 tablespoons of the butter in a heavy-bottomed skillet over medium heat. When the butter is foaming, throw in the shrimp and sauté 4 minutes. Remove the shrimp from the pan and set aside.

Add the remaining butter, chili, garlic and parsley to the skillet. When the butter is foaming, put the shrimp back in the pan and toss 1 to 2 minutes. Season with salt and pepper to taste, add a few drops of lime juice and sprinkle with the lime zest, then serve immediately. Simple and delicious.

One of the great classics of French cuisine—my version is with a hint of the East, something I developed a taste for while working in Singapore. One very important thing with mussels is quality and freshness. A good way to see if you have any bad ones is to wash them in a bowl under running cold water, and if any float to the surface, get rid of them. It is a sign that they are not fresh. As for the rest, remove the beards and wash them until there is not any grit on the bottom of the bowl.

Moules marinières à la citronnelle et au piment

MOULES MARINIÈRES WITH LEMONGRASS & CHILI

Preparation time 15 minutes
Cooking time 6 minutes

4 pounds 8 ounces fresh mussels

1 tablespoon olive oil

2 tablespoons butter

1 shallot, finely chopped

2 tablespoons peeled and thinly sliced gingerroot

1 red chili, seeded and cut into thick slices

2 lemongrass stalks, halved and bruised

4 tablespoons coconut milk

4 tablespoons whipped cream

1 handful of cilantro, leaves only, chopped

sea salt and freshly ground black pepper

Remove and discard the beards from the mussels and wash them in a bowl under cold running water, scrubbing to remove all traces of grit. Discard any that float or any open ones that don't close when tapped.

Heat the oil and butter in a large saucepan over low heat. When the butter begins to foam, add the shallot, gingerroot, chili and lemongrass and cook 2 minutes. Add the mussels and coconut milk and cover the pan. Cook 4 minutes, or until the mussels open. Discard any that remain closed.

Remove the pan from the heat and add the whipped cream and cilantro and season with salt and pepper. Serve immediately, in a large bowl placed in the middle of the table for everyone to share.

Risotto au citron vert

Quiche au Roquefort, brocolis et oignon

Tian de légumes à la Provençale

Tarte à la tomate et au fromage de chèvre

Omelette aux girolles et aux herbes

Ratatouille à la Provençale

Tarte aux artichauts, oignons et thym

Les Plats Végétariens
VEGETARIAN DISHES

The fresh produce in French markets in summer is inspiring. The abundance of fruit and vegetables the warm weather brings makes creating vegetarian recipes easy. You can spread tomatoes in a light pastry case and cover them with goat cheese for a crunchy tomato tart, or layer vegetables in a baking dish with garlic and herbs and create a Provençal Vegetable Gratin. There are risottos, crêpes, vegetable tagines and, of course, the world-famous ratatouille. France often gets a bad press when it comes to vegetarian food, but this is changing and now a selection of vegetarian dishes are often found on brasserie menus.

This colorful Mediterranean dish is ideal for those outdoor summer lunches. Make sure you choose a goat cheese you love. One I really enjoy is Sainte-Maure de Touraine, a chèvre from the Loire region—it is well-balanced, smooth, slightly salty and has a lovely, nutty aroma. Tomatoes are a personal thing, too. Choose the variety that really zings for you. For the topping, you can use your own homemade, oven-dried tomatoes, or, if you are short on time, sun-dried tomatoes from a jar.

Tarte à la tomate et au fromage de chèvre

TOMATO TART WITH GOAT CHEESE

Preparation time 20 minutes, plus making the tomatoes and chilling
Cooking time 50 minutes

butter, for greasing

9 ounces store-bought puff pastry dough

all-purpose flour, for dusting

1 tablespoon balsamic vinegar, plus extra to serve

12 Oven-Dried Tomatoes (see page 41) or 12 sun-dried tomatoes from a jar, drained

3 ounces goat cheese, rind removed, if necessary, and sliced

arugula leaves, to serve

sea salt and freshly ground black pepper

2 tablespoons olive oil, to serve

TOMATO BASE

4 tablespoons olive oil

½ onion, chopped

2 garlic cloves, finely chopped

1 large tomato, chopped

1 thyme sprig

1 tablespoon reduced balsamic vinegar

To make the tomato base, heat 3 tablespoons of the olive oil in a medium saucepan over medium heat. Add the onion and garlic and cook, partially covered, 4 to 5 minutes, stirring occasionally, until soft. Add the tomato, thyme and the remaining olive oil, then reduce the heat to low and simmer 35 to 40 minutes, stirring often to avoid browning or burning the tomatoes. If the mixture gets too dry, add a few tablespoons of water. Stir in the reduced balsamic vinegar and season with salt and pepper.

Meanwhile, heat the oven to 350°F and grease an 8-inch tart pan with a removeable bottom with butter. Roll out the dough on a lightly floured surface until it is about ⅛ inch thick and 10 inches in diameter. Line the pan with the dough, taking care not to stretch it. Press down gently to push out any bubbles and roll the rolling pin along the top edge of the pan to trim off the excess dough. Prick the bottom with a fork and chill 25 to 30 minutes. This prevents the dough from shrinking during baking.

Place the tart pan on a baking sheet and bake 15 minutes, or until golden. Remove the baking sheet from the oven and do not turn off the oven. Brush the pastry with the balsamic vinegar and then return it to the oven 3 minutes. The vinegar seals the top of the pastry and makes it crunchy. Take care not to overbake the crust or it will become dry and bitter.

To assemble the tart, remove the thyme sprig from the tomato base and spread the mixture over the pastry. Arrange the Oven-Dried Tomatoes and goat cheese on top and season with salt and pepper. Place the tart in the oven 3 to 4 minutes longer until the cheese starts to melt, but don't let it melt completely. If you want, you can flash it 2 minutes under a broiler heated to high to give it a lovely color.

Serve sprinkled with rocket and drizzled with oil and balsamic vinegar. *Voilà*—a gorgeous, light and colorful lunch.

Rich, spicy, blue-veined Roquefort is thought to be one of the greatest blue cheeses in the world, and the people of Roquefort protect it fiercely. They have been making it for thousands of years, since the time of ancient Rome, in fact. It proved so popular, imitations of it started to spring up all over the place until, in the 1960s, the *Tribunal de Grande Instance* decreed that, although similar cheeses could be made in many regions of France, it was only a true Roquefort if it had been ripened in the natural caves of Mont Combalou, in Roquefort-sur-Soulzon.

Quiche au Roquefort, brocolis et oignon

ROQUEFORT, BROCCOLI & ONION QUICHE

Preparation time 20 minutes, plus making the dough and chilling
Cooking time 1 hour 10 minutes

1 tablespoon butter, plus extra for greasing

29 ounces Savory Piecrust Dough (see page 23) or store-bought piecrust dough

all-purpose flour, for dusting

2 tablespoons olive oil

1 onion, finely chopped

2 cups broccoli cut into small florets

2 eggs

1 cup heavy cream

¼ teaspoon freshly grated nutmeg

3 ounces Roquefort cheese or other blue cheese of choice, crumbled

sea salt and freshly ground black pepper

salad, to serve

Grease an 8-inch tart pan with a removeable bottom with butter. Roll out the dough on a lightly floured surface until it is about ⅛ inch thick and 10 inches in diameter. Line the pan with the dough, taking care not to stretch it. Press down gently to push out any bubbles and roll the rolling pin along the pan's edge to trim off the excess dough. Prick the bottom with a fork and chill 25 to 30 minutes. This prevents the dough from shrinking during baking.

Meanwhile, make the filling. Heat the butter and oil in a medium skillet over medium heat and cook the onion 10 minutes, stirring occasionally and making sure they don't brown. Remove the pan from the heat and set aside.

Bring a saucepan of salted water to a boil. Add the broccoli and blanch 5 minutes, or until al dente, then refresh in ice-cold water. Drain the broccoli, then pat it dry with a clean dish towel and set aside.

Put the eggs, cream and nutmeg in a bowl, season with salt and pepper and whisk to combine, then set the bowl aside.

Meanwhile, heat the oven to 325°F. When the oven is hot, line the tart with a piece of parchment paper and fill with baking beans. Put the pan on a baking sheet and bake 12 minutes, then remove it from the oven, discard the beans and parchment and turn the oven up to 350°F.

To assemble the quiche, spread the onions over the tart shell. Sprinkle the Roquefort on top, then add the broccoli. Pour in the egg mixture and bake 35 minutes. To check for doneness, do the knife test—it should come out dry and warm. If the quiche isn't ready, return the quiche to the oven 5 minutes longer and test again. When it is baked, set it aside to cool. Remove the quiche from the pan and serve with the salad of your choice. It is delicious warm or cold.

Chanterelle mushrooms are really special. They have a lovely mild flavor and can be picked between late fall and winter. They generally grow under hardwood and softwood trees, especially in older, moss-rich forests. A word of caution—if you decide to go foraging for them yourself, take someone with you who knows what they are doing, or you might end up feeling a bit more special than you hoped, or very ill. If you are in any doubt at all, please don't eat them—you can buy beautiful chanterelles from delicatessens and some supermarkets.

Omelette aux girolles et aux herbes

CHANTERELLE MUSHROOM & HERB OMELET

Preparation time 15 minutes, plus 30 minutes marinating and making the salad
Cooking time 10 minutes

7 ounces chanterelle or cremini mushrooms, trimmed

2 tablespoons olive oil

a few drops of lemon juice

1 tablespoon butter

1 handful of flat-leaf parsley, chopped

1 garlic clove, chopped

8 eggs, beaten

sea salt and freshly ground black pepper

green salad, to serve (optional)

Wash the mushrooms very carefully, because they are fragile and break easily, then pat them dry with paper towels. If the chanterelles are large, just cut them in half, but ideally use small, whole ones. Mix the oil and lemon juice together in a nonmetallic bowl, add the mushrooms and leave to marinate 30 minutes.

Melt the butter in a large, nonstick skillet over medium heat. Drain the mushrooms and sauté them 3 to 4 minutes until they are a nice golden brown, then throw in the parsley and garlic and season with salt and pepper.

Add the eggs to the pan and cook the omelet 3 to 4 minutes until it still has a slightly runny consistency in the middle. Tilt the pan slightly, and, with the help of a wooden spatula, carefully fold over the edge of the omelet, then roll it up. If you prefer your omelet well done, using the spatula, flip it over and cook 3 to 4 minutes longer until pale golden.

Serve the omelet with a green salad, if liked, for a lovely, simple meal.

In France, chanterelles are never on the ground for long—people soon snap them up. But here in Britain, where I now live, people are more nervous about mushrooms being poisonous, so they often perish uneaten. I remember walking through the estate of Castle Kennedy, in Scotland, with my father, where the path was lined with ancient trees and their moisture gave the ground that springy, mossy feeling. Suddenly my father stopped and rushed over to the other side of the path, guarding something fiercely with his body while smiling politely at passers-by, who walked on nervously. He then got down on his knees, took out his penknife and called me over. There on the ground were dozens of chanterelles, their yellow caps a little battered but nonetheless good enough to eat. We cut them, took them home and made an incredible omelet. This recipe, along with my Chanterelle Mushroom & Herb Omelet (page 135) and Wild Mushroom Risotto (page 142), are all close to my heart.

Crêpes aux champignons et estragon

CREPES WITH MUSHROOMS & TARRAGON

Preparation time 15 minutes, plus making the crepes and salad
Cooking time 10 minutes

1 tablespoon olive oil

2¾ cup sliced button and wild mushrooms

1 tablespoon butter

1 handful of tarragon, chopped

1 recipe quantity Basic Crepes, made without sugar (see page 25)

sea salt and freshly ground black pepper

tomato, onion and flat-leaf parsley salad, or arugula salad, to serve

Heat the oven to 350°F. Warm the oil in a nonstick skillet over medium heat and sauté the mushrooms 3 to 4 minutes until the juices they release reduce to a syrup. Add the butter and continue to cook 2 to 3 minutes longer until they are a lovely golden color. Throw in the tarragon and season with salt and pepper.

Lay the crepes on a baking sheet, divide the mushroom mixture over them and roll them up like a wrap. Bake 2 to 3 minutes just to warm through. Serve warm with the salad of your choice.

Les Champignons Sauvages
Wild Mushrooms

As I write this, we are well into fall, my favorite season. Where I lived in Franche-Comté, there are plenty of forests and I used to go there almost on a daily basis when I was growing up—I particularly loved the fall when the trees changed color. My father hunted and often took me with him, although not necessarily to shoot. In fact, we would chat or go on a long walk with our dogs while he told me about the deer. He knew all their habits and could spot them from a few hundred yards—well before I could. He was such a good observer of nature. He had a lot of patience, sometimes waiting for hours at a time just to see the deer. I wasn't surprised when, in his early fifties, my father stopped hunting, but he still took the dogs into the forest for hours. Then, however, he collected mushrooms—and our forest was full of them.

Mushroom pickers are secretive, and we only tell our family or trusted friends where to find the best sources. We worry about people going to the prime location behind our backs, and possibly giving it away to others, which could damage the area. Despite such efforts to keep mushroom locations secret, many people now go foraging. As a result, in France there are now restrictions on how many mushrooms you can pick and, in some areas, guards patrol to check people are respecting the forest.

Very often, I used to go foraging on my own with my dogs. One day just by getting lost on the wrong path, I found I had stepped on a few *trompettes de la mort*, or horn of plenty mushrooms. Suddenly, I looked around and there was a big patch of them in front of me. Generally picked from summer to fall, *trompettes de la mort* are common woodland mushrooms resembling black funnels. They are slightly tough in texture and often chopped and added to a sauce or mixed with other mushrooms. They can also be dried. I like these mushrooms for their very earthy flavor.

Not far away from the *trompettes de la mort*, I also discovered a patch of *girolle* mushrooms (known, too, as chanterelles). Funnel-shaped, *girolles* are found mainly in hardwood and coniferous forests, especially in older, moss-rich forests, and are usually picked between June and October. They are an orange-yellow color with a delicate stem. With their nutty flavor, they are beautiful when pan-fried with herbs and served with pasta. Needless to say, I made sure I marked the spots where these mushroms grew and I returned often to pick more.

There is nothing more satisfying than collecting mushrooms, bringing them home and cooking them. I particularly like *cèpes* (called porcini in Italian) with their large, bulbous stems. They are best eaten young, and are delicious cooked in omelets or velouté sauces. In France, the small ones of the highest quality are known as *bouchons*. There are plenty of *cèpes* here in Britain—for example, in the New Forest—but they can also be bought dried or preserved in oil in jars.

There are also plenty of Scottish *girolles*, which are one inch tall, a bright yellow-orange color and smell like apricots. When we went foraging, Papa and I were on our knees, picking very carefully so the following year's crop would not be compromised. Papa always carried his knife (a hunter's habit, I suppose) folded in his back pocket, along with a plastic bag. I remember holding the *girolles* with bits of moss and leaves still clinging to them, bringing them to my nose and slowly breathing in their incredible scent of earth, apricots, dry leaf, forest and moist soil. Off we went home to prepare them and make the most gorgeous omelet ever. Those are precious memories. It was a brilliant time!

There are hundreds of common mushroom varieties apart from those I've already mentioned, such as button mushrooms and cremini, but some of the tastiest include field mushrooms, *morilles* (morels), oyster mushrooms and blewits. Field mushrooms are found in summer and fall in rich, open, manured grasslands grazed by horses or cows, and are white to pinkish gray with a white stem. These were my Maman's favorite and we used to get up at dawn to collect them. They are delicious sautéed with butter and herbs. Found in springtime, morels are very tasty. Their conical shape has a delightful honeycomb pattern and they have a delicate scent. I like them best cooked with a touch of cream and snipped chives. You can find dried morels in supermarkets and delicatessens. Oyster mushrooms prefer cold weather and are, therefore, found in late fall and winter. They have a very mild flavor and are delicious fricasseed or sautéed with garlic or finished with cream on a steak. And blewits, which are a beautiful lilac color, are found in late fall in pine forests and near hedgerows. They go very well with strongly flavored vegetables, such as onions.

When you go foraging you need to get up as early as possible and just get out and get looking! It is such a satisfying moment when you find a patch of wild mushrooms. And who knows, perhaps you will see a deer or two or other wild creatures on the way, or simply enjoy the colors of the forest and the crunching of the leaves under your feet. Collecting and eating the wrong mushrooms, however, can make you very sick, or even kill you, so before you start, you must learn about them. At first, go foraging with someone who knows what is edible and what is not. Once you have some experience, you can go on your own, but you should still take a good field guide with you, and always double-check you've picked an edible variety. The golden rule is: *if you're not sure, don't eat it.* Prepare wild mushrooms carefully and wash them well. Slugs, snails and other unwanted inhabitants love them, too!

We have local foragers who supply us at The Vineyard, so it's almost as if we had our own patch.

Mushrooms feature in my menu in the late summer, fall and winter on a regular basis, and they're very popular. I prepare them in many different ways, such as in risottos, fricassees and purees; sautéed with herbs in omelets and folded into soufflés. And, of course, they feature in our all-truffle menu, which even includes an ice cream made with the most expensive and highly esteemed of all mushrooms —the black Périgord truffle. This delicacy matures after the first frost and is at its best after Christmas. Truffles are subterranean fungi that live in symbiosis with certain trees, mainly the oak, but also the chestnut, hazel and beech trees. You can now buy them in cans or jars, peeled or scrubbed, ripe, whole or chopped. You can also freeze them. There are several ways of cooking them and they can also be eaten raw if finely sliced.

I don't think I know a chef who doesn't like mushrooms or cooking with them. They are so versatile and go well with many other ingredients, such as fish, shellfish, poultry and meat. Wild game with wild mushrooms is an especially good match —they are made for each other. Mushrooms are also a great option for vegetarians.

Wild mushrooms are readily available during their seasons, and if you don't pick them yourself you can find them in good supermarkets. They are usually also available dried in delicatessens and supermarkets all year round. The flavor, texture and scent of wild mushrooms are very distinct; cultivated mushrooms are more widely available but are no match for the unique appeal of their wild cousins!

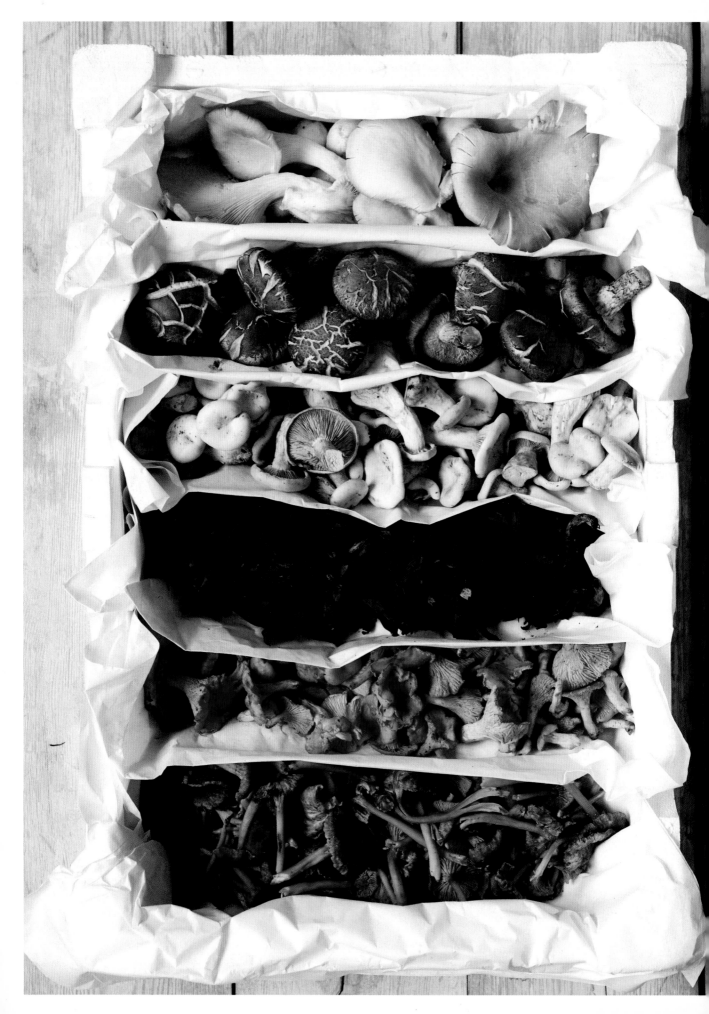

left page from top: **oyster mushrooms, shiitake mushrooms, blewits, horn of plenty, girolles, yellow chanterelles**

right page from top: **cèpes, morilles, cremini mushrooms, button mushrooms**

For this dish, I prefer the *bouchon* mushroom. These are small wild mushrooms, so called because they look like the cork from a champagne bottle. You can buy them dried from a deli, but *cèpes* or porcini mushrooms will also do fine if you can't find *bouchons*. The mistake people often make with a risotto is to think you can leave it—you can't, not even for a single minute, and this recipe is no different!

Risotto aux champignons des bois

WILD MUSHROOM RISOTTO

Preparation time 15 minutes, plus 45 minutes soaking and making the stock
Cooking time 35 minutes

5 ounces fresh *bouchon*, shiitake or porcini mushrooms, or ½ ounce dried porcini mushrooms

½ cup butter

1 large shallot or small onion, very finely chopped

5 tablespoons dry white wine

5 cups Vegetable Stock (see page 19)

1½ cups risotto rice, such as arborio or carnaroli

1 tablespoon crème fraîche

1½ tablespoons snipped chives

sea salt and freshly ground black pepper

Parmesan cheese, to serve

If using fresh mushrooms, wash them very carefully, because they are fragile and break easily, then trim the foot and cut them lengthwise. If using dried mushrooms, soak them in warm water 45 minutes, then rinse and pat dry with paper towels.

Heat 3 tablespoons of the butter in a skillet over medium heat. Add half the shallot and all the mushrooms and sauté 2 minutes, or until golden. Add a few tablespoons of the wine—it will make a great splashing sound—and let it evaporate a little. Season with salt and pepper and set aside.

Now make the risotto. Bring the stock to a boil, then reduce the heat to low and keep it at a simmer.

Melt another 3 tablespoons butter in a large, heavy-bottomed saucepan over low heat. Add the remaining shallot and cook 2 to 3 minutes until soft but not brown, then add the rice and stir. Add the remaining wine and let it evaporate to remove the acidity. Add one ladleful of the stock and stir continuously until it is absorbed. Repeat slowly adding the stock until the rice is cooked, 16 to 18 minutes. The grains should be plump but still firm and not too wet. (Having said that, risotto is a personal thing—I like mine very loose and light.) At the last minute, add the crème fraîche and the remaining butter and finish by folding in the mushrooms and chives and seasoning with salt and pepper.

Serve immediately. Have a hunk of Parmesan cheese and a grater ready at the table in case your guests want to sprinkle some on top. This is truly light and luscious!

If you think of artichokes, it is probably the green ones that spring to mind, but I also like to cook with purple artichokes, which are most often found in Provence. Because they are more difficult to find, they are so often overlooked, which is a pity. They are small and sweet and, when coupled with red bell peppers, bring vibrant color to your dish. Finish the gratin with goat cheese for a scrumptious, seasonal delight.

Gratin d'artichauts et poivrons rouges au fromage de chèvre

ARTICHOKE & RED PEPPER GRATIN WITH GOAT CHEESE

Preparation time 20 minutes
Cooking time 1 hour 30 minutes

juice of 1 lemon

2 large red bell peppers

18 small purple artichokes
  or 11 ounces preserved artichoke
  hearts, drained

4 tablespoons olive oil

2 thyme sprigs

2 garlic cloves, unpeeled and
  crushed with the flat edge
  of a knife or your hand

4 tablespoons dry white wine

1¾ cups heavy cream

4 ounces mild goat cheese,
  crumbled

sea salt and freshly ground black
  pepper

1 teaspoon chopped rosemary,
  leaves only, to serve

Heat the oven to 400°F . Fill a large bowl with water and mix in the lemon juice.

Put the whole peppers on a baking sheet and roast 40 minutes, or until the skins char and wrinkle. Transfer them to a bowl, cover with plastic wrap and set aside 10 minutes, or until the skins loosen and the peppers are cool enough to handle. Using your fingers, peel off and discard the charred skin from the peppers, then seed and cut the flesh into thick slices.

Meanwhile, if using fresh artichokes, remove the outer leaves and cut the tops off. Trim and peel the stems. Cut each in half lengthwise and remove and discard the choke, using a small spoon. Put them immediately in the lemon water to prevent them from discoloring. If you are using preserved artichokes, just drain them thoroughly to get rid of all the oil.

Heat the oil in a medium heavy-bottomed skillet over medium heat. Add the thyme, garlic and artichokes and sauté 3 to 4 minutes, until the artichokes are a light golden color. Add the wine and stir to deglaze, then let it reduce by a third. Season with salt and pepper, reduce the heat to low and simmer, partially covered, 10 minutes. The artichokes should still be firm at this point; they will finish cooking in the gratin. Remove and discard the thyme and garlic, then add the peppers and transfer the mixture to a baking dish and set aside.

Bring the cream to a boil in a small saucepan over medium heat, then reduce the heat to low and simmer 10 minutes. Add the goat cheese and stir until it melts. Season with salt and pepper, then pour this sauce over the artichokes and bake 15 to 18 minutes until the top is pale golden. Serve hot, sprinkled with rosemary.

Tarte aux artichauts, oignons et thym

ARTICHOKE, ONION & THYME TART

*Preparation time 1 hour, plus making
the dough and chilling
Cooking time 50 minutes*

4 teaspoons butter, plus extra
for greasing and if using fresh
artichokes

1 large garlic clove, peeled

9 ounces Savory Piecrust Dough
(see page 23) or store-bought
piecrust dough

all-purpose flour, for dusting

juice of 1 lemon

12 fresh baby artichokes or 8 ounces
preserved artichoke hearts,
drained

3 tablespoons olive oil
(2 tablespoons if using preserved
artichoke hearts)

3 eggs

1 cup plus 2 tablespoons heavy
cream

½ teaspoon freshly grated nutmeg

2 thyme sprigs

3 onions, finely chopped

2 tablespoons grated Parmesan
cheese

sea salt and freshly ground black
pepper

Grease four individual 4½-inch tartlet pans with removeable bottoms, or one 8-inch tart pan, with butter. Rub with the garlic clove, then reserve the garlic. Divide the dough into four balls and roll each ball out on a lightly floured surface until it is about ⅛ inch thick and 6 inches in diameter. (If baking one large tart, roll out the whole quantity of pastry until it is about ⅛ inch thick and 10-inches in diameter.) Line the tartlet pans with the dough, taking care not to stretch it, then press down gently to push out any bubbles and roll the rolling pin over the top edge of the pans to trim off the excess dough. Prick the bottoms all over with a fork and chill 25 to 30 minutes. This prevents the dough from shrinking during baking.

Meanwhile, heat the oven to 325°F. If you are using fresh artichokes, now is the time to prepare them. First fill a large bowl with water and mix in the lemon juice. Remove the outer leaves from the artichokes and cut the tops off. Trim and peel the stems. Cut each one in half lengthwise and remove the choke, using a small spoon, and put it immediately in the lemon water to prevent it from discoloring. Heat 2 teaspoons of the oil and about 1 teaspoon of butter in a skillet over medium heat. Drain the artichokes, then sauté 4 to 5 minutes until golden brown. Remove the skillet from the heat and set aside. If using preserved artichokes, just drain them thoroughly to remove as much of the oil as possible, then set aside.

Put the eggs, cream and nutmeg in a bowl, season with salt and pepper and whisk to combine, then set aside.

Line the tart shells with parchment paper and fill with baking beans. Put them on a baking sheet and bake 12 minutes. Remove the baking sheet from the oven, discard the beans and parchment and turn the oven up to 350°F.

Meanwhile, heat the remaining butter and oil in a medium skillet over medium heat. Add the thyme, reserved garlic and onions and cook gently 10 minutes, stirring occasionally and making sure that the onions don't brown. Discard the thyme.

To assemble the tart, spread the onion mixture over the tart shells, add the artichokes and then pour in the egg mixture. Bake 12 to 15 minutes (20 to 25 minutes for a large tart) until light golden and slightly trembling. Sprinkle with the Parmesan, raise the oven temperature to 425°F and bake 5 minutes longer to give it some color. Ideally serve either hot or warm.

This dish takes time, but it tastes like heaven. Similar to ratatouille, but baked in layers in a baking dish and finished with Parmesan cheese and rosemary, it becomes a tangy, luxuriant meal. If you can get hold of both green and yellow zucchini and red and yellow bell peppers, the dish will be beautifully colorful, too. There are claims that rosemary, besides being powerfully aromatic and delicious, improves the memory and promotes beauty and long life—I'd better get cooking!

Tian de légumes à la Provençale

PROVENÇAL VEGETABLE GRATIN

Preparation time 20 minutes, plus making the eggplant caviar
Cooking time 1 hour 5 minutes

2 large yellow zucchini, cut into long ¼-inch-thick slices

½ cup olive oil

4 rosemary sprigs

2 large red bell peppers

1 recipe quantity Eggplant Caviar (see page 41), made with only 4 garlic cloves

sea salt and freshly ground black pepper

freshly grated Parmesan cheese, for sprinkling

TOMATO BASE

4 tablespoons olive oil

1 onion, chopped

4 garlic cloves, finely chopped

6 tomatoes, chopped

1 teaspoon thyme leaves

1 tablespoon reduced balsamic vinegar

Heat the oven to 400°F. Combine the zucchini slices, oil and rosemary in a bowl and season with salt and pepper, then cover and set aside to marinate.

Meanwhile, put the whole peppers on a baking sheet and roast 40 minutes, or until the skins char and wrinkle. Transfer to a bowl, cover with plastic wrap and set aside 10 minutes, or until the skins loosen and the peppers are cool enough to handle. Using your fingers, peel and discard the charred skin from the peppers, then seed and cut the flesh into long strips.

While the peppers are roasting, make the tomato base. Heat 3 tablespoons of the oil in a medium saucepan over medium heat. Add the onion and garlic and cook, partially covered, 4 to 5 minutes, stirring occasionally, until soft. Add the tomatoes, thyme and the remaining oil, then reduce the heat to low and simmer 35 to 40 minutes, stirring often to avoid burning the tomatoes. If the mixture gets too dry, add a few tablespoons of water. Add the reduced balsamic vinegar and season with salt and pepper.

Heat a cast-iron grill pan, or heavy-bottomed skillet, over medium heat. Drain the zucchini, giving them a shake to get rid of the excess oil, and reserve the rosemary. Grill the zucchini 1 minute on each side, or until they have chargrilled marks. This will give them a lovely color and flavor.

Now you are going to put all the ingredients together. Put half the zucchini slices in a single layer in a flameproof dish. Spread over half the Eggplant Caviar, then cover with half the pepper strips and half the tomato base. Repeat the layers with the remaining ingredients. Chop the rosemary and sprinkle it over the gratin. Bake 20 minutes. Remove the dish the from the oven and turn on the broiler to hot. Sprinkle the gratin with Parmesan and flash it under the broiler 2 to 3 minutes until golden brown, then serve.

I hope you've seen the film of the same name, not just because it's very funny, but also because it is about a passion for great food that's full of flavor—it shows that its namesake dish can satisfy all tastes, from the discerning gourmet to the lover of good home cooking. The word "ratatouille" comes from "*touiller*," which means "to stir round or mix." The recipe originated in Nice, in the South of France, and for me, this dish not only represents but also encompasses the splendor of the South: it is full of sunshine, color and the scent of the Mediterranean.

Ratatouille à la Provençale

RATATOUILLE PROVENÇALE

Preparation time 20 minutes, plus cooking the rice and pasta
Cooking time 2 hours 10 minutes

½ cup olive oil

1 eggplant, peeled and cut into large cubes

1 onion, chopped

4 garlic cloves, crushed

1 red bell pepper, seeded and sliced

1 green bell pepper, seeded and sliced

1 large zucchini or 2 small zucchini, cubed

2¼ cups peeled and seeded tomatoes cut into large cubes

a pinch of sugar

1 bouquet garni made with 1 small handful of flat-leaf parsley sprigs and 1 sprig of thyme, tied together with kitchen string

sea salt and freshly ground black pepper (optional)

a small handful of basil leaves, to serve

rice or pasta, to serve

In a large Dutch oven or cast-iron saucepan, heat the oil over medium heat. Add the eggplant and cook 4 to 5 minutes until soft but not colored. Add the onion, garlic and peppers and cook 2 to 3 minutes longer, stirring occasionally, then stir in the zucchini, tomatoes and sugar. Add the bouquet garni and simmer gently, partially covered, over low to medium heat, 1½ to 2 hours, stirring occasionally. If, when you take the lid off the ratatouille, it is too wet due to condensation, continue cooking it gently with the lid off, until you get the texture and consistency you want.

When ready, check the seasoning and add some salt and pepper, if necessary. Sprinkle with basil and serve with rice or pasta.

CHEF'S TIP: *A lovely way to use up any leftover ratatouille is to mix it with rice and then stuff tomatoes, which you have seeded. Bake them at 350°F 25 to 30 minutes. Or, for a quick snack, top pieces of toasted baguette or a rustic loaf, such as* pain de campagne, *with cold ratatouille. Delicious.*

This is a very special and different risotto, which I normally serve to accompany lamb at The Vineyard—but it tastes wonderful in its own right. Risottos can be done in so many ways: they can be velvety, fragrant, luxurious, elegant or all of these. In this one, the lime brings a refreshing, sharp edge and balances the richness of the cheese and butter beautifully.

Risotto au citron vert

LIME RISOTTO

Preparation time: 15 minutes, plus making the stock
Cooking time: 20 mintues

½ cup butter

1 onion, finely chopped

1½ cups risotto rice, such as arborio or carnaroli

4 cups Vegetable Stock (see page 19), plus extra as needed

1½ limes, zest finely grated with the fruit peeled, cut into segments and chopped, plus extra zest for sprinkling

6 tablespoons grated Parmesan cheese

sea salt and freshly ground black pepper

Heat 3 tablespoons of the butter in a medium skillet over low heat. Add the onion and cook gently 3 to 4 minutes, stirring occasionally, until light golden. Add the rice and turn the heat down to very low. Mix with a wooden spoon until the rice is well coated with the butter and onion.

Add the stock, little by little, stirring continuously until the liquid is absorbed before adding more stock. Carry on adding stock, stirring until absorbed after each addition, until the rice has a lovely, creamy texture. Make sure the risotto does not stick to the bottom of the pan.

At the last minute, stir in half the chopped lime segments, the lime zest, Parmesan and the rest of the butter. Place the remaining lime segments, covered, in the refrigerator to use another day. If the risotto is too thick, add a few more spoonfuls of stock to loosen it up, then season with salt and pepper, sprinkle with extra lime zest and serve immediately.

Couscous, made from husked, crushed semolina wheat, is very much a North African dish. It has become popular in France, however, and is now frequently found on brasserie menus. The type of couscous dish you find in France will differ according to the region you are in, what produce is available at the time of year and how spicy you like it. I prefer mine milder and more aromatic than spicy, which is what I have offered here. Also, I like to use the *moyen*, or medium-size, grain.

Couscous de légumes et pois chiches

VEGETABLE & CHICKPEA COUSCOUS

Preparation time 30 minutes, plus making the stock
Cooking time 40 minutes

3 tablespoons olive oil

2 zucchini, cut in half lengthwise and then into pieces

2 carrots, peeled and sliced

2 turnips, peeled and cut into wedges

1 onion, roughly chopped

1 teaspoon four-spice mix (including ground ginger, nutmeg, cloves and white pepper)

a pinch each of cayenne pepper, ground coriander and ground cumin

1 teaspoon coriander seeds

4¼ cups Vegetable Stock (see page 19)

2 tablespoons tomato paste

1 cup medium-grain couscous

4 tablespoons butter

¾ cup canned chickpeas, drained and rinsed

sea salt and freshly ground black pepper

a handful of cilantro, leaves only, chopped, to serve

Heat 2 tablespoons of the oil in a medium skillet over medium heat. Add the zucchini, carrots, turnips and onion and sauté 5 minutes, or until the vegetables are pale golden. Stir in the spices, stock and tomato paste and cook over low heat 30 minutes, partially covered and stirring occasionally, until the vegetables are tender but still have some bite to them.

When the vegetables have cooked about 15 minutes, put the couscous in an heatproof bowl and set aside. In a medium saucepan, put one-third of the butter and 1 cup water, season with salt and pepper and bring to a boil. Pour the liquid over the couscous, mixing with your other hand. Cover the bowl of couscous with plastic wrap and let stand 10 minutes, or until the couscous is tender. Meanwhile, add the chickpeas to the vegetables and heat through.

Remove the plastic wrap and fluff up the couscous with a fork. Add and stir in the remaining butter, little by little, then season again with salt and pepper. Drizzle the remaining oil over and sprinkle with cilantro. Serve the couscous with the vegetables, spooning some of the liquid from the vegetable pan over the top.

Chou braisé

Épinards au beurre et citron

Frisée aux lardons

Haricots verts au beurre et échalottes

Fondant de pommes de terre à l'ail confit

Pommes de terre sautées persillées

Gratin de pommes de terre au vieux comté

Les Accompagnements et Salades
SIDE DISHES & SALADS

I always look forward to the change of seasons and how that is reflected on our plates, especially when it comes to side dishes and salads. Each season brings its own special selection of the fresh, the earthy, the tender, the robust and the sweet—something for every mood, every day. Whether steamed, sautéed, roasted, baked or broiled and tossed with olive oil or butter, or served in a salad with a tasty dressing—the possibilities are endless. There is always something delicious and new to enjoy.

Courgettes à l'huile d'olive et thym

ZUCCHINI WITH OLIVE OIL AND THYME

Preparation time 5 minutes, plus
15 minutes marinating
Cooking time 10 minutes

4 zucchini, cut into long
    ¼-inch-thick slices

4 tablespoons olive oil

1 teaspoon thyme leaves

sea salt and freshly ground black
    pepper

Heat the oven to 350°F. Combine the zucchini slices, oil and half the thyme in a bowl and season with pepper. Set aside to marinate a good 15 minutes, so the herbs can work their magic.

Heat a cast-iron grill pan over medium to high heat. Spread the zucchini across the lines of the pan and cook 3 minutes on each side until slightly soft but still retaining some bite. You will need to work in batches, depending on the size of your pan.

Transfer the zucchini to a baking sheet, sprinkle with sea salt, a little more pepper and the rest of the thyme leaves. Place them in the oven 3 to 4 minutes to finish cooking, then serve.

Haricots verts au beurre et échalottes

BUTTERED GREEN BEANS WITH SHALLOTS

Preparation time 10 minutes
Cooking time 10 minutes

14 ounces green beans, trimmed

2 tablespoons butter

1 shallot, finely chopped

sea salt and freshly ground black
    pepper

Bring a saucean of salted water to a boil and blanch the beans 4 to 5 minutes until al dente, then refresh in a bowl of ice-cold water. Drain well and pat dry with paper towels.

Melt the butter in a skillet over medium heat. Add the green beans and shallot and cook 2 to 3 minutes until slightly al dente and well coated with butter. Season with salt and pepper and serve.

Chou braisé

BRAISED CABBAGE

Preparation time 5 minutes
Cooking time 5 minutes

1 savoy cabbage, outer leaves
    removed

4 teaspoons butter or 2 tablespoons
    olive oil

2 tablespoons finely diced carrot

sea salt and freshly ground black
    pepper

Cut the cabbage in half, then core and slice it very thinly. Bring a large saucepan of lightly salted water to a boil and blanch the cabbage 1 to 2 minutes, then drain. Rinse it under cold water to keep the color, then pat it dry with paper towels and set aside.

Using the same pan you blanched the cabbage in, melt the butter over low heat. When it is foaming, throw in the cabbage and carrot and cook 2 to 3 minutes, stirring occasionally, until tender. Season with salt and pepper and serve.

Petits pois à la Française

PEAS WITH PANCETTA & ROMAINE LETTUCE

Preparation time 10 minutes
Cooking time 40 minutes

2 tablespoons butter

12 pearl onions, peeled

1 teaspoon sugar

¼ cup pancetta, cut into
    ¼-inch-thick strips

1 tablespoon olive oil

4 cups fresh shelled peas

1 romaine lettuce, torn into pieces

sea salt and freshly ground black
    pepper

Bring a small saucepan of water to a boil. Melt the butter in another small saucepan over medium heat. When it is foaming, throw in the onions and cook 4 to 5 minutes, stirring occasionally, without browning. Season with salt and pepper, then add enough water to cover the onions and cook 15 minutes, or until the onions are soft and the liquid reduces by half. Add the sugar and cook, stirring, 3 to 4 minutes until the onions are glazed, transparent and shiny, then set aside.

Add the pancetta to the pan of boiling water and blanch 1 to 2 minutes, then refresh in cold water, drain and pat dry. Heat the oil in a skillet over medium heat and sauté the pancetta 7 to 8 minutes until crisp and golden brown, then set aside.

Add the peas and romaine lettuce to the pan with the onions and simmer, stirring occasionally, 3 to 4 minutes. The peas should be tender, the onions still whole and the lettuce just a little crunchy. Add the pancetta and season with salt and pepper. Serve hot.

Walking in the countryside of France, you could be forgiven for thinking this purple thistle is little more than a weed. But you'd be missing something really special. Catherine de Medici, an Italian princess, recognized this plant for the delicacy it is, and was responsible for bringing it to France in the sixteenth century.

Artichauts violets braisés à la citronnelle, roquette et parmesan

BRAISED PURPLE ARTICHOKES WITH LEMONGRASS, ARUGULA & PARMESAN

Preparation time 35 minutes
Cooking time 25 minutes

juice of 1 lemon

16 small purple artichokes
   or 10 ounces preserved artichoke
   hearts, drained

2 tablespoons olive oil

4 garlic cloves, crushed with the flat
   edge of a knife or your hand

2 lemongrass stalks, halved and
   bruised

1 lemon, halved

⅔ cup dry white wine

1 small red bell pepper, peeled if
   desired, seeded and chopped

sea salt and freshly ground black
   pepper

3 ounces arugula leaves, to serve

1¾ ounces Parmesan or other hard
   cheese, such as Comté, shaved,
   to serve

DIJON MUSTARD DRESSING

1 teaspoon Dijon mustard

2 tablespoons olive oil

1 tablespoon balsamic vinegar

If using fresh artichokes, fill a large bowl with water and mix in the lemon juice. Remove the outer leaves from the artichokes and cut the tops off, then trim and peel the stems. Cut each one in half lengthwise and put them immediately in the lemon water to prevent them from discoloring.

Heat the oil in a heavy-bottomed saucepan over medium heat. Drain the artichokes and add them to the pan. Cook 3 minutes, turning occasionally with a wooden spoon, until golden brown all over. Add the garlic and lemongrass and squeeze a few drops of lemon juice over, then cook 5 minutes longer. If using preserved artichoke hearts, cook 1 minute before adding the garlic, lemongrass and lemon juice and then 2 minutes longer.

Add the wine, season lightly with salt and pepper and continue cooking 2 to 3 minutes until it reduces slightly, then add the red pepper. Reduce the heat to low and simmer, partially covered, 10 minutes, or until the liquid reduces by at least half, 2 to 3 tablespoons. The artichokes should be cooked but still very firm. Remove the artichokes and red pepper from the pan and set aside 15 minutes. If there is any remaining cooking liquid in the pan, strain it into a small bowl and discard the lemongrass.

Meanwhile, make the dressing. Add the mustard, oil and balsamic vinegar to the cooking liquid. Season with salt and pepper and whisk to combine.

When the artichokes are cool, scoop out and discard the chokes, using a small spoon. Be careful not to lose any of the artichoke heart just below the choke. Cut the flesh into quarters, if preferred.

Arrange the artichokes on a plate, top with the arugula, red pepper and Parmesan shavings, sprinkle with the dressing and serve. This is a delicious, refreshing and colorful dish, and also makes a great accompaniment to broiled or grilled meat or fish.

The secret with frisée lettuce is to choose one that is really yellow. You need to use all the yellow and only the top section of the light green part. Discard the rest, which can be very bitter. Try keeping the frisée in cold water 20 minutes before preparing this dish to make it extra firm and crunchy. This salad is delicious served alongside an omelet and sautéed potatoes.

Frisée aux lardons

FRISÉE WITH PANCETTA

Preparation time 10 minutes
Cooking time 15 minutes

5 ounces pancetta, cut into ½-inch dice

2 tablespoons sunflower oil

1 teaspoon Dijon mustard

2 tablespoons red or white wine vinegar or balsamic vinegar

½ cup olive oil

1 yellow frisée lettuce, torn into bite-size pieces

sea salt and freshly ground black pepper

Bring a saucepan of water to a boil and blanch the pancetta 1 to 2 minutes, then refresh in cold water, drain and pat it dry. Heat the sunflower oil in a skillet over medium heat. Add the pancetta and sauté 8 to 10 minutes until crisp.

In a small bowl, mix together the the mustard, vinegar and 2 tablespoons water, then whisk in the olive oil until the mixture is very thick and glossy. Season with salt and pepper.

Put the frisée in a bowl, toss with the vinaigrette and add the crisp pancetta, then serve.

Epinards au beurre et citron

BUTTERED SPINACH WITH LEMON ZEST

Preparation time 15 minutes
Cooking time 35 minutes

zest of 1 lemon, cut into thin strips

1 tablespoon superfine sugar

2 tablespoons butter

1 garlic clove, chopped

1 pound 2 ounces large leaf spinach, well rinsed

sea salt and freshly ground black pepper

Bring a small saucepan of water to a boil and blanch the strips of lemon zest 4 to 5 minutes to soften and to get rid of any chemicals. Drain and refresh in cold water, then drain, blanch and refresh again. Put the sugar in the pan with enough water to just cover and stir to dissolve. Add the zest and simmer 20 minutes, or until glazed. The lemon strips should be candied, shiny and not sticking to each other. Set the strips of zest aside.

Heat the butter in a medium saucepan over medium heat—it needs to be hot enough for the spinach to wilt quickly, but not so hot that the butter burns! Add the garlic and spinach and cook 2 minutes until it wilts. Season with salt and pepper, then drain and squeeze off any excess liquid.

Serve hot sprinkled with the candied lemon zest.

Pommes de terre persillées

SAUTÉED POTATOES WITH PARSLEY & GARLIC

Preparation time 10 minutes
Cooking time 20 minutes

3 cups new potatoes cut into
  ¼-inch-thick slices

2 tablespoons sunflower oil

2 tablespoons butter

1 small handful flat-leaf parsley,
  roughly chopped

1 garlic clove, chopped

sea salt

Bring a medium saucepan of salted water to a boil. Add the potatoes and blanch 8 minutes, then drain and pat dry with paper towels.

Warm the sunflower oil in a large skillet over medium heat. Add the potato slices and cook 3 to 4 minutes on each side until golden brown. Just before the potatoes are ready, add the butter and let it melt around them—it will give them an extra crispiness and a nutty flavor. At the last minute, throw in the parsley and garlic and sprinkle with salt. Serve immediately.

Écrasée de pommes de terre à la coriandre et citron vert

WARM CRUSHED POTATOES WITH CILANTRO & LIME

Preparation time 10 minutes
Cooking time 15 minutes

14 ounces new potatoes

juice and zest of 1 lime

1 small handful of cilantro, leaves
  only, roughly chopped

olive oil, for drizzling

sea salt and freshly ground black
  pepper

Bring a large saucepan of salted water to a boil and boil the potatoes 8 to 10 minutes until tender but still slightly firm. Drain, refresh under cold water and peel, then crush slightly with a fork—not too much or you will turn them into mashed potatoes.

Season with salt and pepper, then add the lime juice and zest and the cilantro. Drizzle with a little oil and serve.

Fondant de pommes de terre à l'ail confit

FONDANT POTATOES WITH CONFIT OF GARLIC

*Preparation time 15 minutes, plus
making the stock
Cooking time 35 minutes*

1 tablespoon sunflower oil

7 tablespoons butter, chopped

1 pound 2 ounces small waxy
potatoes, peeled

8 garlic cloves, unpeeled and
crushed slightly with the flat edge
of a knife or your hand

scant ½ cup Vegetable Stock (see
page 19) or Chicken Stock
(see page 18)

1 rosemary sprig

sea salt and freshly ground black
pepper

Heat the oven to 350°F. Put the oil and butter in a baking dish. Add
the potatoes and garlic and bake 15 to 20 minutes until golden brown
all around.

Add the stock and rosemary and bake 15 minutes longer, or until the stock
is absorbed and the potatoes are soft and garlicky. Season with salt and
pepper and serve.

Gratin de pommes de terre au vieux comté

POTATO GRATIN WITH AGED COMTÉ

*Preparation time 10 minutes
Cooking time 50 minutes*

scant 1 cup whole milk

scant 1 cup heavy cream

1 teaspoon freshly ground nutmeg

1 bay leaf

1 garlic clove, cut in half

4 tablespoons butter

3 cups thinly sliced floury potatoes

1 heaping cup grated aged Comté
cheese or other mature hard cheese

sea salt and freshly ground black
pepper

Heat the oven to 275°F. Put the milk, cream, nutmeg and bay leaf in a
medium saucepan over medium heat and season with salt and pepper.
Bring to a boil, then remove the pan from the heat and discard the bay leaf.

Rub a flameproof baking dish all around with the garlic clove, then grease
it with the butter. Arrange the sliced potatoes in the dish. Stir half the
cheese into the milk mixture and pour it over the potatoes. Sprinkle the
remaining cheese on top, then bake 45 minutes, or until the cheese melts
and is lightly colored.

Meanwhile, heat the broiler to high. Broil the gratin 3 to 4 minutes until
golden brown. Serve immediately.

Grosses frites au sel de mer

LARGE FRENCH FRIES WITH SEA SALT

Preparation time 20 minutes, plus
1 to 2 hours chilling
Cooking time 45 minutes

2¼ pounds floury potatoes, peeled
    and thickly sliced

1 quart sunflower oil

sea salt

Bring a large saucepan of salted water to a boil. Cut off both ends of the potatoes, then peel them and cut them into large, long fries, about 3/4 inch thick. Wash them to get rid of any excess starch. Drop the fries into the boiling water 6 to 8 minutes. They should still be very firm when you drain them. Line a tray with paper towels, then drain the potatoes carefully, so you do not to break them, and put them on the tray. Leave them to cool, then chill them 1 to 2 hours.

Heat the oil in a large saucepan over low heat to 275°F. If you don't have a thermometer, you can check the temperature by dropping a piece of potato in—if it floats and bubbles, the oil is hot enough. Add the potatoes in 2 or 3 batches, depending on the size of your pan, and fry 4 to 6 minutes until firm but not colored. Remove the fries from the oil with a slotted spoon and set aside to drain on a tray lined with paper towels. Repeat with the remaining potatoes.

When ready to serve, increase the temperature of the oil to 360°F. Fry the fries again in batches 4 to 6 minutes until they are a lovely golden color. Serve hot sprinkled with salt.

Purée de pommes de terre à la crème

CREAMED MASHED POTATOES

Preparation time 30 minutes
Cooking time 55 minutes

2¼ pounds floury potatoes,
    unpeeled

7 tablespoons whole milk

7 tablespoons heavy cream

2 garlic cloves, sliced

sea salt and freshly ground black
    pepper

Heat the oven to 400°F. Wash the potatoes thoroughly, then add them to a large saucepan, cover with water and add a pinch of salt. Bring to a boil, then lower the heat and simmer 30 to 40 minutes until completely cooked through. Drain quickly and place the potatoes on a baking sheet. Put the potatoes in the oven 10 minutes, then remove them and peel.

While still warm, quickly pass the potatoes through a strainer or food mill. Do not let them cool, or the mixture will be gluey; cover and set aside.

Put the milk, cream and garlic in a saucepan and bring to a boil. Remove the pan from the heat and pour half the liquid mixture over the potato mixture. Mix well, then add the rest of the liquid, little by little. Season with salt and pepper and serve hot.

I find potato salad can be a bit heavy, which is why I love to put plenty of herbs in it. Sorrel and chervil are beautiful herbs, but can be tricky to find; market stalls are your best bet. Wild sorrel is found alongside rivers and in wetlands in the springtime —it looks like an elongated spinach and tastes very bitter. If you can't find chervil, use extra chives or some tarragon instead. I like to use vinaigrette rather than mayonnaise, because it keeps potato salad light and refreshing. This is a great one for picnics.

Salade de pommes de terre nouvelles aux oeufs durs et vinaigrette au Xérès

NEW POTATO SALAD WITH HARD-BOILED EGGS & SHERRY VINAIGRETTE

Preparation time 20 minutes
Cooking time 30 minutes

2¼ pounds new potatoes

1 fennel bulb, 2 to 3¼ inches long

1 teaspoon vinegar

2 eggs

sherry vinegar, for drizzling

1 small handful of spinach leaves, trimmed

1 small handful of sorrel leaves, trimmed (optional)

1 small handful of mixed lettuce leaves

6 chervil sprigs, finely chopped

2 mint leaves, finely chopped

5 dill sprigs, finely chopped, plus extra to serve

2 scallions, finely chopped

1 tablespoon roughly snipped chives

4 radishes, thinly sliced

sea salt and freshly ground black pepper

SHERRY VINAIGRETTE

1 teaspoon Dijon mustard

1 tablespoon sherry vinegar

3 tablespoons olive oil

Bring a large saucepan of salted water to a boil. Add the potatoes and fennel and simmer over medium heat 30 minutes, or until both are tender.

Meanwhile, hard-boil the eggs. Fill a small saucepan with water and bring to a boil. Add the teaspoon of vinegar to the water, because this makes the eggs easier to shell after cooking. Place each egg in a ladle, then slowly and carefully slide the egg into the water so you don't break the shell. Cook 8 to 9 minutes, then drain and place the eggs under running cold water. When cool enough to handle, shell the eggs, cut in quarters and set aside.

Drain the potatoes and fennel and refresh under cold water. Peel the potatoes, then cut the potatoes and the fennel into thick slices. Put them in a bowl and drizzle with some sherry vinegar.

Arrange the spinach, sorrel and lettuce on a large serving dish, leaving a space in the middle for the potatoes and fennel. Sprinkle the chervil, mint, dill, scallions and chives over the greens, then season with salt and drizzle with more sherry vinegar. Put the potatoes and fennel in the middle of the dish and arrange the eggs around them.

To prepare the vinaigrette, put the mustard, vinegar and oil in a bowl and season with salt and pepper. Whisk to combine, then pour the dressing over the potato salad.

Sprinkle with extra dill sprigs and the radish slices and serve.

Les Herbes

Herbs

I cannot remember a day when there weren't any herbs in my home or my kitchen, and if such an instance ever were to happen, it would be purely by accident. Would I be able to cook without them? Yes, because I love my trade. Would I like it? Probably not.

It is very difficult to explain how essential herbs are to the cooking process or how profoundly they enhance food, whether added to a salad, meat, fish, vegetables or even a dessert. They have such an important place in the kitchen simply because they bring so much taste, so much scent, so much color to a dish.

If I close my eyes for a few minutes, I can remember what it was like in my childhood when you could smell a wonderful scent of herbs floating around the house when Maman was cooking. It's easy to recall the fragrance of herbs in the freshness of spring or the height of summer, or in your garden, at the market stall or on vacation somewhere like Provence. There, such vast quantities of so many different herbs grow that the sheer intensity of their scent can be overwhelming and disorienting to the senses. Imagine, if you can, herb fields stretching as far as the eye can see and the sweet scent of thyme mixed with juniper or lavender. What an amazing pleasure, what a delight and what a landscape!

Rather than taking center stage and overpowering a dish, I think herbs are best used in the background, as a subtle finishing touch that really completes a dish. The herbs I've selected for use in the recipes in this book are mostly common and easily available, so you can enjoy cooking with them. I have carefully matched them with each recipe for a well-balanced effect.

Like everyone, I have a few favorite herbs I often use. One of them is thyme, one of the most versatile and commonly used herbs in the kitchen.

It is especially good with meats, such as pork, lamb and mutton, because it aids the digestion of fats (one reason it is also used as a tisane to revitalize the spirit and refresh the senses), and it's also used in stuffings, ragouts and, of course, the all-essential bouquet garni —my standard bouquet garni is made up of a sprig of thyme, a sprig of parsley and a bay leaf.

Another herb I like to use is lavender. Many people do not associate lavender with cooking and are surprised to find it in food, but it is a versatile culinary herb. It is great in meat and poultry dishes, as well as desserts. We use it in our specialties at The Vineyard. Lavender infused in honey and chili, for example, gives a wonderful flavor to fish dishes. Lavender is everywhere in Provence, with fields full of row after row of purple flowers. The scent invades the whole area—you can smell it in stores, restaurants, cupboards, bathrooms and, of course, in perfumes. It can sometimes be a little overpowering, but, used carefully, the scent and taste of lavender is a pure delight.

Other herbs mentioned in the recipes in this book include parsley, chives, tarragon, chervil, cilantro, sage, mint, lemongrass, dill and sorrel. The first four of the herbs I mentioned above are also the main ingredients of *fines herbes*, a staple of French cuisine. In that herb mixture they are chopped very finely and usually added right at the end of the cooking process.

Another interesting herb that I recommend you try is *sarriette*, or winter savory, which is great in soups, with vegetables or, again, in desserts. Winter savory can be difficult to find, but it is worth tracking it down. For me, it really comes into its own when it is paired with fava beans.

While I'm on the subject of pairings, I should mention there are many complementary relationships between herbs and other ingredients that seem made in heaven—for example, chicken with fresh thyme, duck with lavender, and, of course, lamb with rosemary.

You may be wondering how I could have left off my list so far a herb as important as rosemary, but really, I was simply saving my favorite until last. At home, I rarely cook without rosemary. While it's difficult to explain why I love it so much, I suspect it is partly because it is so evocative of my childhood, reminding me of when I would cut it freshly from our garden at home to go in whatever dish Maman was preparing that day. The smell of rosemary stays on your hand for a while, then, unnoticed, it disappears. But it never leaves you really—instead it stays and wafts around in your memory all your life.

Rosemary has beautiful light purple or white flowers that blossom twice a year. These can be eaten, like many other flowers, including thyme and winter savory, as well as nasturtiums and pansies, which are often included in salads or used as decoration.

When mixed with other ingredients, rosemary changes character. It is a great herb, but its strength can be lethal, and adding too much of it can make a dish taste bitter. Using rosemary carefully is, therefore, crucial—but when you succeed, you have a heavenly scent. Make the Tarte Tatin with Rosemary and Toasted Almonds (see page 180) and you will discover how rosemary lifts the apples and mixes with the sugar so well. Or, use this versatile herb in a lamb dish, such as Roast Lamb with Mediterranean Vegetables & Sauce Vierge (see page 67) to bring out its many flavors, or skewered in a pineapple to add depth.

Rosemary also has a connection with the great English writer, William Shakespeare, as it is mentioned in several of his plays. Each year on Shakespeare's birthday, branches of rosemary are carried in the streets of Stratford-upon-Avon. What a great day that must be!

Tied with rosemary as a firm favorite is another perhaps less well-known herb—chervil. Again, it is a herb that Maman used a lot, especially in soup. When the soup was almost ready, she would chop the chervil quickly, then just throw it in and serve. At that point, as the scent of the herb made contact with the heat, the magic began for me, and I'll always remember the way the enticing aroma gradually wafted around and drew me in. I could never resist a second helping, both because of the chervil scent and because the soup was great, too. Chervil has a slightly peppery taste and it goes especially well with buttered carrots, lifting and enhancing their flavor. Unfortunately, chervil can be difficult to find in stores, but you can always make sure you have a plentiful supply by growing it yourself in spring or summer in your garden or in a pot on the windowsill.

In fact, growing a variety of herbs in your very own herb garden, whether in your kitchen or on a balcony, a roof terrace or a windowsill, is a great idea, especially if you cook a lot. Not only does this allow you to control the quality of the herbs you use in your cooking (after all, you nurtured those plants yourself), but it also means that you regularly get to use fresh herbs, whose flavor is completely different from and far superior to the flavor of store-bought dried herbs.

I've expounded at length here and only scratched the surface of the fascinating world of herbs. If you'd like to learn more, I suggest that you begin by following the recipes in this book to get a better idea of how to use them. Then, your understanding of the role herbs play in the kitchen will expand quickly.

Once you have a basic knowledge and feel confident enough, start experimenting with using herbs in different ways and with new herbs you discover for yourself. I guarantee you won't regret it.

clockwise from top left:
flat-leaf parsley, sorrel, mint,
sage, cilantro, rosemary,
chives, chervil, dill

These salads were two of my favorites when I was young, and ones that are very common to find on brasserie display counters. Fresh and easy to serve, they are simple, yet delightfully tasty salads; if you have freshly picked carrots from your own garden, the second recipe is simply the best—it goes very well with any terrine.

Salade de concombre à la moutarde de Dijon et ciboulette

CUCUMBER SALAD WITH DIJON MUSTARD & CHIVES

Preparation time 25 minutes, plus 20 minutes resting and making the vinaigrette

1 cucumber, peeled and cut into ⅛-inch-thick slices

1 tablespoon French Vinaigrette (see page 20)

1 tablespoon heavy cream

1 teaspoon Dijon mustard

1 small handful of chives, snipped

sea salt and freshly ground black pepper

Put the cucumber in a large bowl and sprinkle it with salt. Mix well, then set aside 15 to 20 minutes to let the cucumber release its juices.

Rinse the cucumber quickly under running cold water to remove the excess salt, then pat dry with a clean dish towel.

Mix together the vinaigrette, cream and mustard and season with salt and pepper. Pour the dressing over the cucumber, sprinkle with the chives and serve immediately.

Salade de carottes râpées au cerfeuil

GRATED CARROT SALAD WITH CHERVIL

Preparation time 15 minutes, plus making the vinaigrette

3 carrots, peeled and coarsely grated

2 tablespoons French Vinaigrette (see page 20), or to taste

1 small handful of chervil or cilantro, leaves only, chopped

sea salt and ground white pepper

Put the carrots in a large bowl. Stir in the vinaigrette, adjusting the amount you use to taste, season with salt and white pepper and sprinkle with the chervil.

Serve chilled as an appetizer.

There are lots of different onions, but none as good as the lovely sweet white onions from the South of France, which are for me the perfect partners to bring this tomato salad to life. Here, I pair the French white onion with flat-leaf parsley, but you can use red onion and basil instead. Just don't use the large Spanish onion, which has a different flavor, texture and purpose. With a sprinkling of freshly cut herbs, along with olive oil, red wine vinegar, garlic and a touch of salt and pepper, you have the perfect summer salad. Get your baguette ready to dip into those juices and wonderful dressing!

Salade de tomates aux oignons

GARDEN TOMATO & ONION SALAD

Preparation time 15 minutes

4 large ripe Italian plum tomatoes or round garden tomatoes, cored and cut into ¼-inch-thick slices

4 small tomatoes, quartered

4 small yellow tomatoes, halved

1 small white onion or 1 large scallion, white part only, thinly sliced

4 tablespoons olive oil

2 tablespoons red wine vinegar

2 tablespoons balsamic vinegar

1 handful of flat-leaf parsley, chopped

1 garlic clove, finely chopped

sea salt and freshly ground black pepper

sliced baguette, to serve (optional)

Arrange the tomato slices, quarters and halves on a serving dish and sprinkle the onion over them. Season with salt and pepper and drizzle with the oil and vinegars, then top with the parsley and garlic. Enjoy as a salad, with sliced baguette, or as a side dish.

Tarte au citron et zest de citron vert

Mousse au chocolat noir et zest d'orange

Clafoutis à la framboise

Tarte aux fruits rouges et citron vert

Crème au café caramelisée

La tarte aux pommes de Maman

Crêpes soufflées à l'orange

Les Desserts

DESSERTS

My grandparents' orchard produced so much fruit Grand-Père had to think up ingenious ways to store it. I used to pick the fruit (although more went in my mouth than in my basket), and Grand-Père wove the storage baskets himself. He then filled them with juicy apples, layered with hay, and stored them in the attic, then when that was full, he put them in the cellar. They kept beautifully right through to the spring, enabling us to make wonderful desserts, such as Maman's Apple Tart. The next problem was where to put the apricots, pears, cherries, red currants … Apricot Tart and Summer Fruit Tart with Lime are just two delicious examples of how we enjoyed them.

Phyllo pastry packages are great because you can put almost any fruit you like in them and end up with a fabulous dessert bursting with flavor. (Just make sure that the fruit isn't too ripe or it will soak the pastry.) These little packages can be as fragrant, as sweet or as spicy as you like: add citrus zest, nuts and the spices of your choice. Work quickly and keep the dough covered with a damp cloth to prevent it from drying out. Served warm and crunchy with a delicate fruit sauce or coulis, these taste like heaven.

Parcelles de fruits

FRUIT PACKAGES IN PHYLLO PASTRY

Preparation time 30 minutes
Cooking time 15 minutes

14 ounces phyllo pastry dough sheets

all-purpose flour, for dusting

7 tablespoons butter, melted

11 ounces mixed berries or the fruit of your choice, hulled and prepared as necessary

2 vanilla beans, cut in half lengthwise

4 petals of 1 star anise

1 teaspoon freshly crushed black peppercorns

3 tablespoons superfine sugar

zest of 1 lime

confectioners' sugar, for sprinkling

ice cream or 1 recipe quantity Vanilla Custard Sauce (see page 24) to serve

Heat the oven to 350°F. Unroll the phyllo pastry dough, spread it out on a lightly floured work surface and cut it into 16 rectangles, each about 12 x 6 inches. Brush each dough rectangle with some of the melted butter, stacking one on top of the other to create 4 stacks of 4 dough rectangles. By coating each piece of dough in butter, you will get a beautifully crumbly package. It also prevents the pastry from becoming soggy when the fruit releases its juices during baking.

Leaving a 1¼-inch-wide border along the edges, arrange your fruit selection in the middle third of each dough stack, keeping the remaining dough free to fold over. Top each portion of fruit with half a vanilla bean and 1 star anise petal and sprinkle with the black pepper, sugar and lime zest.

Working with one dough-and-fruit stack at a time, brush the edges of the dough again with some of the remaining butter. Fold the right-hand side of the dough over to cover the fruit, then fold the left-hand side over to cover the dough and fruit. Gently pinch the open top and bottom edges together and tuck them under to make sure the package is well sealed. Repeat until you have assembled 4 packages, using all the fruit.

Transfer the packages onto a greased baking sheet and sprinkle with confectioners' sugar, which will create a lovely glaze during baking. Bake 15 minutes, or until golden brown and shiny. Serve warm with ice cream or Vanilla Custard Sauce.

CHEF'S TIP: *Crumble 1 or 2 amaretti cookies over the fruit mixture in each package before folding them up. This adds a subtle almond flavor to the filling and the crumbs also soak up the fruit juices to help keep the pastry crisp.*

This classic dessert carries the name of the two famous Tatin sisters, who invented the recipe. Everybody loves it, I think, because of the smell of warm apple mixed with caramel, and the delicious crunchiness of the light pastry. Just add the contrast of cold crème fraîche or ice cream and you have one of the most fabulous, yet simple, desserts on the planet. Personally, I like it with a touch of rosemary—when you open the oven door you are enveloped in the incredible perfume of rosemary-scented apples. The scent alone is a miracle worth waiting for!

Tarte tatin au romarin et amandes grillées

TARTE TATIN WITH ROSEMARY & TOASTED ALMONDS

Preparation time 15 minutes, plus chilling
Cooking time 1 hour

8 ounces store-bought puff pastry dough

all-purpose flour, for dusting

½ cup sugar

3 tablespoons unsalted butter

1 rosemary sprig, leaves only, roughly chopped

3 or 4 apples, such as Golden Delicious, Cox or Reinette, peeled, quartered and cored

a large pinch of toasted slivered almonds, plus extra for sprinkling

crème fraîche, to serve

Roll out the dough on a lightly floured surface, then cut out a circle slightly bigger than an 8-inch flameproof baking or tatin dish. Roll the dough over the rolling pin and place it on a baking sheet, cover with plastic wrap and chill the dough 25 to 30 minutes. This will prevent it from shrinking during baking.

Heat the oven to 375°F. Melt the sugar gently in the baking or tatin dish over medium heat until golden brown, then remove it from the heat and stir in the butter. Sprinkle about one-quarter of the rosemary leaves over. Arrange the apples tightly along the edge of the dish in a circle, then make smaller circles of tightly fitted apples within this circle until the bottom is covered and all the apples are used. Bake 35 minutes.

Remove the baking dish from the oven, sprinkle the remaining rosemary and the almonds over the apples and place the dough on top, tucking the edge into the side of the dish. Return the dish to the oven and bake 20 minutes longer, or until the pastry is golden brown and crisp.

Remove the tart from the oven and leave it to cool for a few minutes. Put a large upturned plate on top of the tart and, holding both the plate and dish, flip them over, giving a firm shake halfway, to unmold the tart onto the plate. Sprinkle with a few extra almonds. *Et voilà*—a perfect tarte tatin with rosemary. Enjoy while warm. I think this is delicious served with chilled crème fraîche.

What used to amaze me about the apples my grandparents grew and stored on the farm was that, even if the skin was as wrinkled as Grand-Père's face, the inside stayed fresh and beautiful—just like him, he used to say! Even after months of storage, the taste was tremendous. So with these apples, my Grand-Mère taught Maman to bake. With these apples, Maman taught me to bake. Whenever I tell my son, Antoine, we are going to visit his Grand-Mère in France, the first question he asks is, "Can you ask her to bake an apple tart, please, Papa?"

La tarte aux pommes de Maman
MAMAN'S APPLE TART

Preparation time 30 minutes, plus making the pastry and chilling
Cooking time 25 minutes

1 extra-large egg

7 tablespoons heavy cream

3 heaping tablespoons sugar

butter, for greasing

1 recipe quantity Grand-Mère's Sweet Tart Dough (see page 22), Sweet Piecrust Dough (see page 22) or 8 to 9 ounces store-bought piecrust dough

all-purpose flour, for rolling out the dough

2 tablespoons finely ground blanched almonds

4 or 5 apples, such as Crispin or Jonagold, peeled, cored and cut into wedges

Mix the egg, cream and sugar in a bowl, beating with a whisk or electric mixer 5 minutes, or until fluffy.

Grease a 9½-inch loose-bottomed tart pan with butter. Roll out the dough on a lightly floured surface until it is ⅛ to ¼ inch thick, about 11 inches in diameter. Roll the dough over the rolling pin and place it over the tart pan. With one hand lift the dough edge and with the other gently tuck the dough into the bottom and side of the pan so it fits tightly. Don't overstretch it or it'll break, and press down gently to push out any bubbles. Trim off any excess dough by rolling the pin over the top edge of the pan. Prick the dough on the bottom all over with a fork, cover with plastic wrap and chill 25 to 30 minutes.

Toward the end of the chilling time, heat the oven to 350°F. Place the tart pan on a baking sheet and sprinkle the ground almonds over the tart bottom. Arrange the apple pieces in a fan shape over the almonds, starting from the outside edge and finishing in the middle. Arrange the pieces as regularly as you can. Pour the egg mixture over the apples, making sure the whole surface is covered with the mixture and there are not any gaps.

Bake the tart 20 to 25 minutes until pale golden. Remove the tart from the oven and set aside until it cools down a little.

Serve the tart while it is still a little warm, when it is most delicious. You don't need ice-cream—it's best on its own with a lovely cup of espresso on the side to sip!

L'Epiphany on January 6 is a big event in France. On that day, we traditionally serve a dessert called *la galette des rois*—a delicious layered *feuilleté*, or light puff pastry, filled with frangipane almond cream. Another tradition is to hide a coin in the dessert and whoever finds it (without breaking his or her teeth, we hope) gets the crown and is king or queen for the day. The recipe here is a twist on the classic. I use an almond cream that's similar to frangipane, then add apricots and finish it off with toasted almond slivers. It's one of my favorites for texture as well as flavor.

Tarte à l'abricot
APRICOT TART

Preparation time 30 minutes, plus making the pastry, chilling and cooling
Cooking time 45 minutes

½ cup finely ground blanched almonds

4 tablespoons sugar

1 egg, beaten

a few drops of vanilla extract

4 tablespoons whipping cream

4 tablespoons butter, soft, plus extra for greasing

1 recipe quantity Sweet Piecrust Dough (see page 22) or 8 to 9 ounces store-bought piecrust dough

all-purpose flour, for dusting

1¾ pounds ripe apricots, halved and pitted

¼ cup smooth apricot jam

½ cup slivered almonds, toasted

Put the ground almonds, sugar, egg, vanilla extract, cream and half the butter in a bowl and mix until you have a lovely, smooth almond paste, then set aside.

Grease a 9½-inch loose-bottomed tart pan with butter. Roll out the dough on a lightly floured surface until it is ⅛- to ¼-inch thick, about 11 inches in diameter. Roll the dough over the rolling pin and place the dough over the tart pan. With one hand lift the dough edge and with the other gently tuck the dough into the bottom and side of the pan so it fits tightly. Don't overstretch it or it'll break, and press down gently to push out any bubbles. Trim off any excess dough by rolling the pin over the top edge of the pan. Prick the pastry bottom all over with a fork, cover with plastic wrap and chill 25 to 30 minutes.

Toward the end of the chilling time, heat the oven to 350°F. Place the tart pan on a baking sheet and spread the almond paste over the bottom. Arrange the apricot halves on top like a rose window. To do this, arrange the apricots along the edge of the tart so they are slighly overlapping, then make smaller circles of overlapping apricots within this circle until the bottom is covered and all the apricots are used.

Bake the tart 30 minutes, then check to see if the apricots are soft, the pastry is pale golden and the almond cream is firm to the touch. If the tart needs more time, bake 5 to 10 minutes longer. (The apricots will need more time if they are less than ripe). Remove the tart from the oven and set aside to cool 15 minutes.

Melt the apricot jam in a small saucepan over low heat, then brush it over the top of the tart. Sprinkle with slivered almonds and serve slightly warm—the temperature makes all the difference.

In Alsace, there is a village named Turckheim. It has the charm of many French villages, with its cobbled streets, small stores and a fountain into which so many are anxious to throw their coins. This one stands out in my memory because of the lamplighter, who, every evening at 10 o'clock, strolls the streets in traditional costume, lighting lamps, singing songs and calmly announcing the hour. My father used to go wine tasting there and, as we were still a bit young for wine (even by French standards), my mom would take us to a *pâtisserie*, where we gorged on summer fruit tart with berries so fresh they made our lips and teeth purple.

Tarte aux fruits rouges et citron vert

SUMMER FRUIT TART WITH LIME

Preparation time 30 minutes, plus making the crème pâtissière , chilling and cooling
Cooking time 25 minutes

1 egg yolk

9 ounces store-bought puff pastry dough

all-purpose flour, for dusting

reduced balsamic vinegar, for brushing

½ cup Crème Pâtissière (see page 24) or thick custard sauce

zest of 1 lime

juice of ½ lime

⅓ cup strawberries, halved and hulled

½ cup blackberries

½ cup raspberries

⅓ cup blueberries

¼ cup smooth raspberry jam

Line a baking sheet with parchment paper. In a small bowl, beat the egg yolk with 1 tablespoon water and set aside. Roll out the dough on a lightly floured surface—the thickness will already be fine, you just need to roll it so you can cut out a 12- x 6-inch rectangle. Reserve the leftover dough trimmings.

Roll the pastry over the rolling pin and place it on the baking sheet. Brush the edges with the egg yolk mixture, then use the leftover dough trimmings to make a small border, 1/2 inch wide, all around the rectangle. The border makes sure your Crème Pâtissière and fruit won't run off the sides later. Brush the top of the border with the egg yolk mixture, prick the dough bottom all over with a fork, cover with plastic wrap and chill 25 to 30 minutes.

Heat the oven to 350°F. Bake the pastry shell 20 minutes, or until light brown, then remove the baking sheet from the oven and transfer to a cooling rack. Brush the bottom of the pastry with the reduced balsamic vinegar (this helps to make it crisp) and leave to cool. Meanwhile, put the Crème Pâtissière, lime zest and half the lime juice in a bowl and mix well.

Spread the cream mixture over the pastry case and arrange the fruit in lines on top, alternating to create a colorful pattern.

Melt the jam in a small saucepan over low heat, then brush it over the fruit to glaze. Sprinkle with the remaining lime juice and leave to set in a cool place 30 minutes, then serve.

Tarte au citron et zest de citron vert

LEMON TART WITH LIME ZEST

Preparation time 20 minutes, plus making the pastry and chilling
Cooking time 1 hour 15 minutes

1 cup plus 2 tablespoons lemon juice

1¼ cups sugar

zest of 2 limes

7 eggs

1 cup plus 2 tablespoons heavy cream

butter, for greasing

1 recipe quantity Grand-Mère's Sweet Tart Dough (see page 22), Sweet Piecrust Dough (see page 22) or 8 or 9 ounces store-bought piecrust dough

all-purpose flour, for rolling out the dough

Put the lemon juice and ¾ cup of the sugar in a small saucepan over medium heat and cook, stirring, 8 to 10 minutes until the sugar dissolves and the liquid reduces. Remove the pan from the heat, add the lime zest and set aside.

Beat the eggs and the remaining sugar in a large bowl, using an electic mixer or whisk, 3 to 4 minutes until the mixture is fluffy, pale yellow and starting to form ribbon-like shapes when you lift the beaters and it falls back into the bowl. Add the lemon mixture and cream and whisk to combine. Cover with plastic wrap and leave to infuse 1 hour in a cool place but not the refrigerator.

Meanwhile, grease a 9½-inch loose-bottomed tart pan with butter. Roll out the dough on a lightly floured surface until it is ⅛- to ¼-inch thick. Roll the dough over the rolling pin and place the dough over the tart pan. With one hand lift the dough edge and with the other gently tuck the dough into the bottom and side of the pan so it fits tightly. Don't overstretch it or it'll break, and press down gently to push out any bubbles. Trim off any excess dough by rolling the pin over the top edge of the pan. Prick the bottom all over with a fork and chill 25 to 30 minutes. This will prevent it from shrinking during baking.

Toward the end of the chilling time, heat the oven to 325°F. Place the tart pan on a baking sheet, line the tart shell with a piece of parchment paper and fill with baking beans. Bake 15 minutes, then remove the baking sheet from the oven, remove the beans and parchment paper and turn the oven down to 200°F.

Strain the lemon mixture into a medium saucepan and warm it through over low heat, as gently as possible, stirring continuously. This gives the filling a headstart in the oven—a cold filling would have to bake much longer.

Pour the filling into the pastry case and bake 40 to 45 minutes until set. It should tremble slightly when the tart is gently shaken before removing from the oven. Leave to cool completely before cutting to serve.

CHEF'S TIP: *If you want to give the tart a twist, sprinkle confectioners' sugar on top and broil it briefly to give it a brûlée look and add an extra wow factor. This tart needs little adornment, but you can serve with it with raspberries, a fruit coulis or ice cream.*

Les Fromages
Cheeses

Probably the most widely eaten individual food in the world, cheese is a great source of protein and comes in a stunning variety of names, shapes and packaging. It is one of the most ancient forms of man-made food and references to cheese-making are dotted throughout ancient literature. Even in ancient Sumerian texts dating from 3,000bc, there are references to "twenty soft cheeses."

For me, cheese is an essential part of the dining experience, and no meal is complete without it. In this book, you will find many recipes containing cheese. Almost all of them are French, but Italian Parmesan is also mentioned in some places.

Cheese is very popular in my home region of Franche-Comté, which is especially well known for *Comté*, one of the most famous and widely eaten cheeses in France. *Comté* is one of the few products apart from wine to be granted AOC (*Appellation d'Origine Contrôlée*) status, which guarantees the quality and authenticity of the product and protects it from imitation. There are only 42 cheeses, two butters and one cream that are part of this elite. *Comté* is the most popular cheese in France—about 40 percent of the population consume it, which is an enormous number. Made with cow milk (45% minimum fat content), it is cooked and pressed. *Comté* is ivory colored or pale yellow and has a fruity flavor and a strong bouquet. Categorized as a hard cheese and referred to as "cooked," *Comté* is made by heating the milk during production. It is unusual, as the milk has only to reach 104°F, therefore it is an unpasteurized cheese, made with *lait cru*, or raw milk, as opposed to pasteurized cheese, which is "cooked" at 162°F 20 to 30 seconds like, for example, *Ossau-Iraty* (see opposite). Maman always prepared a *Comté* sandwich for us when we came back from school. We absolutely loved the afternoon treat of slices of the cheese in baguette.

Every morning, we would have another cheese for breakfast, again with baguette. This time it was *Cancoillotte*, a cheese, interestingly, that is made from another cheese, *metton*, which comes in both factory-produced and handmade varieties. To make *Cancoillotte*, the *metton* is melted with water or milk, a pinch of salt and a small quantity of butter. It's served hot on potatoes or spread cold on bread. I love it, and every time I go to visit Maman, she makes some for us—it is such a delicious treat and it instantly whisks me back to my childhood. *Metton* is made from skim milk, which is coagulated, thinly cut and heated to 140°F, then pressed, pounded and ripened for a few days.

Another cheese from my region is also a big name: *Vacherin Mont d'Or*. It is seasonal and everyone awaits it with great anticipation. Made from the summer milk high in the Massif du Mont d'Or, this cheese is packaged and ripened in a wooden box and bound by a band of spruce bark, which lends it a distinct flavor. After three weeks at a maximum of 61°F, it is cured on a board of spruce wood, and turned, then rubbed with a cloth soaked in brine. The imprint of the cloth gives the cheese a unique appearance.

Before moving on from my region's cheeses, I want to mention *Morbier*, another outstanding product protected by a special AOC label of origin. It is a cow-milk cheese (45% fat content), which is traditionally made by layering the curd from the morning's milk on top of that from the evening's milk, with a protective layer of ash in between. It is best in spring, as it is made with the winter milk production from the chalets of the foothills. It has a creamy interior with a dark line through the middle.

Of course, it is not only my region in France that produces great cheeses, the whole country does. Let me tell you about a few of my favorites. I am a big fan of *Fourme d'Ambert*, a cow's milk blue cheese that comes from the Loire and the Puy de Dôme (45% fat content). Holding AOC status, it has a firm interior flavored with parsley, and a dry, gray crust mottled with yellow and red. It has a strong flavor and is shaped into a tall cylinder. Another cheese I like very much is *Époisses*, a soft cow-milk cheese named after a village on the Côte d'Or and made in almost every part of Burgundy. It also contains 45 percent fat and has an orange washed crust (done first with sage, then with a Burgundy brandy). At its best in winter, *Époisses* is creamy inside and has a very strong flavor.

My next recommendation is *Livarot*, a full-bodied cow-milk cheese (45 to 50% fat content) from the Calvados region of Normandy. It has a soft, smooth inside and a washed brown-red rind. Traditionally tinted with annatto (fruit from a tropical flowering tree), this rich cheese is farm made and also carries an AOC label. The best time to eat it is from November to June. And finally, the last of my favorites—*Fougerus*: a sumptuous cow-milk cheese from the Île-de-France, which has a soft interior and a whitish rind (55% fat content). It is similar to *Brie* but smaller and has fern leaves wrapped around its rind. There is also a variety without the leaves, which is known as *Coulommiers*.

Something happened a few years back, without my noticing. I still don't know why, but I found myself more and more drawn toward pungent goat- and sheep-milk cheeses. As we mature, so does our palate, and perhaps I am now more appreciative of the complexity and strong flavor of these cheeses than I was before, when they were always on our table at home. I would like to share some particularly special ones with you. One of my favorite sheep-milk cheeses is *Ossau-Iraty*, from the Pyrenées region (50% fat content). It has a creamy, yellow, lightly pressed curd, a smooth orange-yellow rind and a pronounced nutty flavor. It has AOC status and is

great as a snack, on canapés or in a salad. I love *Crottin de Chavignol*, a goat-milk cheese made in the Sancerre region that contains at least 45 percent butterfat. It has a soft center and a natural crust mottled with white, blue or brown mold. This cheese can be eaten when it is freshly made and very mild, or savored after it has ripened for three months, at which point it is crumbly and more piquant. I also really like *Sainte-Maure de Touraine*, a soft, white goat-milk cheese with AOC status. It is shaped like a log and has a slightly nutty flavor with a distinctive gray, moldy rind. This cheese contains 45 percent fat and has an unusual feature—a piece of straw running through the middle, which leaves a slight dry-hay aftertaste and reminds me of harvest time. Another of my favorite goat cheeses is *Pouligny-Saint-Pierre*, from the Berry region. It has a smooth curd and a fine natural rind with a bluish tinge. Also awarded AOC status, it has a strong flavor and is shaped like a pyramid. It is best from April to November.

Nowadays, we are very lucky, because in many countries, as in France, more and more fabulous regional cheeses are being crafted by passionate producers on their own small farms. I'm sure you'll agree, we must protect and support them, and recognize their efforts to bring us the best possible natural products by buying from them directly, or from markets. For me, this is what it is all about —being able to choose and be recommended that special cheese, handmade traditionally and passed down through generations, not made in a factory where there is no soul, no history, no passion.

The recipes in this book will help you to start your journey to explore the vast range of cheeses available. But you cannot serve cheese without its best friend—wine. What a match, what a duo, what a great end to a meal! Why not turn them into a great meal on their own by serving them with warm, fresh bread—surely there is nothing better!

left page clockwise from top
left: Coulommiers, Morbier, Vacherin
Mont d'Or, Époisses, Forme d'Ambert,
Pouligny-Saint-Pierre, Crottin de
Chavignol

right page clockwise from top:
Fougerus, Livarot, Sainte-Maure de
Touraine, Ossau-Iraty, aged Parmesan,
aged Comté

Suzanne was actually my great aunt, but I think her cakes alone were enough to earn her the title of *Grand-Mère!* She always used to say it was the quality of the farm eggs that made them taste so good—the yolks were a deep orange color—and they gave her cakes such lightness and flavor. My father loved going to Grand-Mère's. The first thing he did when he got there was look for the cakes. Grand-Mère liked to hide them so she could tease us that she hadn't baked any, but we always knew she had because of the incredible aromas wafting around the kitchen.

Le gâteau de Suzanne

SUZANNE'S CAKE

Preparation time 20 minutes
Cooking time 40 minutes

⅔ cup butter, slightly melted, plus extra for greasing

4 cups all-purpose flour, plus extra for dusting

8 eggs

½ cup sugar

a pinch of salt

1 cup plus 2 tablespoons crème fraîche

2 teaspoons baking powder

confectioners' sugar, for dusting

Heat the oven to 350°F. Grease an 8½-inch cake ring pan with butter and dust it with flour.

In a large bowl, whisk the eggs, sugar and salt together until frothy. Add the crème fraîche and butter and mix with a wooden spoon until it is all incorporated and the batter is smooth. Add the flour and baking powder and keep mixing until it is smooth again. Pour the batter into the pan and bake 40 to 45 minutes until the tip of a sharp knife inserted into the middle comes out hot and dry.

Switch the oven off, open the door slightly and leave the cake inside for 8 to 10 minutes longer so it settles without sinking. Remove the cake from the oven and turn out onto a wire rack to cool. To serve, carefully transfer to a serving plate and dust with confectioners' sugar. Simple and delicious!

Originating in the Limousin region, clafoutis soon spread throughout France to become a popular dessert in brasseries all over the country. Traditionally, a clafoutis is made with cherries, but the summer brings an abundance of fruit—tender apricots, juicy plums, fat cherries and wild blackberries, all warm from the sun and begging to be eaten. You can make a delicious clafoutis with any of these, but my favorite is raspberry. The sweetness of the berries and the zing of the lime zest send your taste buds twirling!

Clafoutis à la framboise

RASPBERRY CLAFOUTIS

Preparation time 35 minutes
Cooking time 25 minutes

2 to 2¼ cups firm raspberries

zest of 1 lime

½ cup sugar

4 tablespoons butter, half soft and
half melted

⅔ cup all-purpose flour

a pinch of salt

1 egg

1 egg yolk

1¼ cups whole milk

Heat the oven to 350°F. Put the raspberries, lime zest and 2 tablespoons of the sugar in a bowl. Mix gently, then set aside to macerate 15 minutes. Meanwhile, grease a 9½- x 6¼- x 2½-inch baking dish or clafoutis dish (an oval earthenware dish) with the soft butter and sprinkle with another 3 tablespoons of the sugar. Carefully shake the sugar around the dish to make sure it coats the inside.

Sift the flour and salt into a mixing bowl. In a separate bowl, whisk together the egg, egg yolk and remaining sugar, then slowly add this mixture to the flour and mix until incorporated and smooth. Slowly add the milk, stirring until the batter has the consistency of a crêpe batter, then add the melted butter and mix until combined.

Put the raspberries in the clafoutis dish and mix to release their juices. Pour the batter over the raspberries, then bake 25 minutes until golden brown and set. A tip of a sharp knife inserted into the middle should come out clean and dry. Remove the clafoutis from the oven and serve.

CHEF'S TIP: *It is also fun to make this dessert in individual ⅔-cup ramekins. Follow the recipe above and just reduce the cooking time to 10 to 12 minutes.*

Sunday evening is a favorite time for making crêpes in our house, and orange soufflé crepes are a fantastic change to the plain crepe served with sugar or jam, and a delicious treat. The soufflé mixture, placed in the top pocket of the folded crepe, is sweet, sharp, light and utterly sublime.

Crêpes soufflées à l'orange

ORANGE SOUFFLÉ CREPES

Preparation time 30 minutes, plus resting and making the custard
Cooking time 1 hour

1¼ cups milk

½ vanilla bean

1 cup all-purpose flour

2 tablespoons vanilla-flavored sugar

a pinch of salt

2 eggs

juice and grated zest of ½ orange

1 tablespoon orange liqueur, such as Cointreau or Mandarin Imperial

3 tablespoons butter, melted, plus extra for frying, if needed

confectioners' sugar, to serve

ORANGE SOUFFLÉ MIXTURE

4 egg whites, beaten

scant ¼ cup sugar

2 tablespoons Vanilla Custard Sauce (see page 24)

juice and grated zest of ½ orange

In a small saucepan, warm the milk over low heat 2 to 3 minutes. Scrape the vanilla seeds into the warm milk, add the pieces of the vanilla bean and leave to infuse 30 minutes. Discard the vanilla bean.

Put the flour, vanilla sugar, salt, eggs, orange juice and zest and liqueur in a bowl. Add one-third of the milk mixture and the melted butter and whisk until smooth. Alternatively, just pop it all into a blender if that's easier for you and blend 2 to 3 minutes. Slowly whisk or blend in the remaining milk. Make sure that there are not any lumps in the batter and the consistency is very runny so your crêpes will be thin and light. If you make the batter gradually like this, you won't have to let it rest.

Heat a 6- to 7-inch nonstick crepe pan or a nonstick skillet over medium to high heat. (Using a nonstick pan means you won't have to add butter before cooking the crepes, as you already have some in the batter, although, of course, it can make flipping the crepes easier if you do.) Using a ladle, put enough batter in the pan to cover the bottom thinly, tilting the pan, if necessary. Cook 1 to 1½ minutes. Now comes the fun part—try to flip it. Use a spatula, however, if you want to stay on the safe side. Cook 1 to 2 minutes longer on the second side, then transfer the crepe to a plate and set aside at room temperature. Continue to make 12 to 15 crepes in total.

Heat the oven to 400°F. To make the soufflé mixture, put the egg whites and sugar in a bowl and beat with an electric mixer 8 to 10 minutes (or whisk by hand) until firm. Put the custard in another bowl and whisk in half the egg-white mixture to make a smooth paste, then fold in the remaining egg white mixture. It should be silky but firm.

Fold each crepe in half, then in half again. Put them on a nonstick baking sheet, making sure they're not too close together so they have room to grow. Lift the top layer of each crepe and spoon the soufflé mix into it. Bake 8 to 10 minutes until the crepes rise like a soufflé but stay firm. Remove the baking sheet from the oven, dust with confectioners' sugar and serve immediately. Once you start eating these, you'll never want to stop!

Luxurious, smooth crème caramels—make these in the morning and they'll be set and ready in time for dinner. It's worth it just to see the look on your guests' faces when you appear with a blowtorch to finish them off. (The crème caramels that is, not the guests!) I've made them here with coffee, but you can replace the coffee with many other flavorings and spices, such as vanilla, cinnamon, chocolate, lemongrass and star anise.

Crème au café caramelisée
COFFEE CRÈME CARAMEL

Preparation time 15 minutes, plus
*   4 hours chilling*
Cooking time 1 hour

heaping ¾ cup sugar

1 cup plus 2 tablespoons milk

7 tablespoons heavy cream

3 tablespoons instant coffee
    granules

3 eggs

2 egg yolks

3 tablespooons soft brown sugar,
    to caramelize (optional)

Have ready four ²/₃-cup ovenproof pots (or six smaller pots if you want to serve smaller portions). Put ½ cup of the sugar in a small heavy-bottomed saucepan and melt over medium heat, stirring with a wooden spoon until it melts and turns a pale caramel color. Immediately pour it into the pots and swirl them around to coat the bottoms and sides with the hot caramel. Use a dish towel to protect your hands. Set the pots aside and leave to cool completely.

Heat the oven to 225°F and line a deep baking dish with waxed paper. The paper will direct the bubbles away from the pots, providing a more gentle cooking process so the custard doesn't curdle. Combine the milk, cream, coffee granules and ¼ cup of the sugar in a saucepan and gently bring to a boil over low heat, stirring to dissolve the sugar and coffee. In another bowl, whisk together the eggs, egg yolks and remaining sugar 1 to 2 minutes until pale and the sugar dissolves. Pour the boiling milk mixture into the egg mixture, whisking as you go.

Divide the mixture into the pots and put them in the baking dish, then pour enough warm water into the dish to come halfway up the sides of the pots (this is called a bain-marie). Put the baking dish in the oven and bake 45 minutes, or until the tip of a sharp knife inserted into the middle of a pot comes out clean. If necessary, return the baking dish to the oven and cook 5 to 10 minutes longer. Remove the dish from the oven and transfer the pots to a wire rack to cool completely. Cover with plastic wrap, then refrigerate at least 4 hours.

I like to caramelize the creams just before serving. If you want to do this, you will need a bit of courage and a blowtorch! Sprinkle the tops of the pots with the brown sugar and caramelize with the blowtorch for a few seconds. If you haven't got a blowtorch, you can pop them under a hot broiler about 1 minute.

Everyone needs a little chocolate in their life, or so my wife Claire tells me. The combination of chocolate and orange is one of my son's favorites, too, so this dessert never lasts long in our house. You'll need a good-quality chocolate for this: I recommend 66 to 70 percent pure cocoa, which has a slight bitterness and a hint of spice. One thing, though, watch out for the chocolate disappearing: it seems to evaporate in our house whenever my back is turned!

Mousse au chocolat noir et zest d'orange

BITTER CHOCOLATE MOUSSE WITH ORANGE ZEST

Preparation time 20 minutes, plus
1 hour chilling
Cooking time 20 minutes

1 orange

6 tablespoons sugar

3½ ounces bittersweet chocolate
(66 to 70% cocoa solids),
chopped into small pieces

3 egg yolks

⅔ cup heavy cream

1 tablespoon confectioners' sugar

Pare the zest from the orange into fine strips using a zester or a small, sharp knife, cutting any pith away. Put the zest in a small saucepan, cover with cold water and bring to a boil over medium heat. As soon as it starts to boil, remove the pan from the heat. Refresh the zest under cold water and drain, then repeat this entire process once more.

Using the same pan, return the zest to the pan and add 2 tablespoons of the sugar and 3 tablespoons water, stirring to dissolve the sugar. Bring to a boil and cook 4 to 5 minutes until the zest becomes transparent. Leave the zest strips to cool in the syrup. When cold, drain and set aside.

To make the chocolate mousse, put 2½ ounces of the chocolate in a heatproof bowl and rest it over a saucepan of gently simmering water, making sure the bottom of the bowl does not touch the water. Heat 4 to 5 minutes, stirring occasionally, until the chocolate melts, then remove from the heat and keep warm. In a separate heatproof bowl, mix together the remaining sugar, egg yolks and 2 tablespoons warm water. Rest the bowl over the saucepan of simmering water, making sure the bottom of the bowl does not touch the water. Beat the mixture 8 to 10 minutes until it turns pale, thickens and forms ribbon-like shapes when you lift the whisk and the mixture falls back into the bowl. Slowly stir in the melted chocolate until well combined.

In another bowl, whip the cream and confectioners' sugar until soft to medium peaks form, then gently fold it into the chocolate and egg mixture until you obtain a lovely, smooth mixture, taking care not to overmix it. Divide the mousse into four glasses, glass dishes or large ramekins. Cover the four dishes with plastic wrap and chill 1 hour before serving. If chilled for longer, remove from the refrigerator 30 minutes before serving. Just before serving, melt the remaining chocolate in a heatproof bowl over simmering water. Use a small spoon to swirl the chocolate around each mousse, then top with the orange zest and serve.

This is one of my favorite desserts—I just love the intriguing contrast between the cold, creamy custard and the brittle, hot layer of caramelized sugar. For me, crème brûlée is particularly delicious served with a fruit puree—raspberry and blackberry are both sensational. They bring the perfect acidity needed to balance the richness—just as you're being lulled into luxury by the sugar and cream, a sharp burst of summer fruit explodes in your mouth. It's a wonderfully decadent treat.

Crème brûlée à la purée de framboises

CRÈME BRÛLÉE WITH RASPBERRY PUREE

Preparation time 30 minutes
Cooking time 50 minutes

4 egg yolks

⅓ cup sugar

1 cup plus 2 tablespoons heavy cream

2 tablespoons soft brown sugar, for sprinkling

RASPBERRY PUREE

1 cup raspberries

grated zest of 1 lime

2 tablespoons sugar

First make the raspberry puree. Put the raspberries, lime zest and sugar in a bowl and mix gently using a fork. Set aside to macerate about 15 minutes, then crush the mixture into a puree, using a fork. There's no need to pass it through a sieve as you want to keep the seeds to give the puree more flavor.

Heat the oven to 300°F and line a deep baking dish with waxed paper. The paper will direct the bubbles away from the pots, providing a more gentle cooking process so the custard doesn't curdle. Whisk the egg yolks and sugar together in a heatproof bowl until smooth. Gently heat the cream in a saucepan over low heat, then slowly pour it into the egg yolks, whisking as you go. Make sure it is smooth with no lumps, otherwise you'll end up with scrambled egg.

Divide the puree equally into four ⅔-cup ramekins, then divide the egg and sugar mixture equally into the ramekins and put them in the baking dish. Pour enough warm water into the dish to come halfway up the side of the ramekins (this is called a bain-marie). Place the baking dish in the oven and bake 35 to 40 minutes until set but still slightly trembling when shaken. Remove the dish from the oven and transfer the ramekins to a wire rack to cool until set.

Heat the broiler to high. Sprinkle the brûlées with the brown sugar and put them on a baking sheet. Broil 2 to 3 minutes until the sugar caramelizes. Serve immediately.

INDEX

AUTHOR ACKNOWLEDGMENTS

I would like to thank the following people:
My family, for all their support and friendship; my suppliers: Eric Charriaux at Premier Cheese, Martin at Channel Fisheries, the Bread Factory, and John Piper at Oakleaf Ltd.; Jane and her team, for providing me with a Thermomix, to help with some of the recipes—it's a great tool; The Vineyard management, my head chef, Frédéric, and the rest of my team for allowing me time out to do the book and photoshoots; my agent, Rosemary Melbourne, for her support; the team at the HHB Agency, especially Heather Holden-Brown, for her constant support and cheerful nature, and for putting up with me.

I also want to thank my publishers: Duncan, Grace, Manisha, Camilla and the rest of the gang for their enormous patience, for having faith in me and for their guidance to see the project through; the photographer Yuki, for her wonderful talent, her

sense of humor and for keeping me on track; Aya, my assistant, who's a great cook and lots of fun, and who bosses me around (with good reason!)—it's super to work with her; Heston Blumenthal for his foreword, his friendship and for always being such a gentleman; James Martin for sending me such a lovely note and for being my friend; and my dad, Daniel Senior, for passing on to me all his passion and respect for nature. And, finally, two very special people: my son Antoine, for being who he is—beautiful, funny, and loving life and food; and my wife Claire, for being there throughout the project and helping me to translate from my "franglais" into lovely, readable text. Without her, her patience, her friendship and her Italian charm, it would have been a much bigger challenge.